Gutsy Glorious Life Coach

How to Turn Your Life Coaching Practice into a Soulful Money-Making Business

by Lin M. Eleoff, Esq.

Gutsy Glorious Life Coach: How To Turn Your Life
Coaching Practice Into A Soulful Money-Making Business

DISCLAIMER: The information contained in this book is
intended as reference material only. It is your responsibility to
practice due diligence and to make informed decisions when it
comes to launching, growing, and protecting your online
business.

Cover design by Rhianon Paige and Martin Velesci

Interior design by Abigail Michel

Project and release managed by The Solution Machine

www.TheSolutionMachine.com

ISBN: 978-0-9832868-1-3

Printed in the United States of America

For Stephen,

with love,

always and forever.

And to the children we love with all our hearts,

Brooklin

Dylan

MacKenzie

Rhianon

And to all the coaches who put so much heart and soul into

their work...

This is your time.

AUTHOR'S NOTE

Dear Coach,

I've packed a lot of information into the pages that follow. I implore you to not just read it all but to actually *do it all*. To help you take action I've created a **step-by-step action checklist** of everything (as in, *every*-thing) you'll need to do in order to launch, grow, and *protect* your online business, even the legal stuff (because, hey, I'm a life coach *and* a lawyer!).

I call this checklist "**The 46 STEPS**."

You can download the checklist for free at GutsyGloriousLifeCoach.com.

Questions? Send an email to info@lineleoff.com.

TABLE OF CONTENTS

INTRODUCTION:
BUSINESS JUST GOT REAL

So. You're a life coach.

You're committed to making a difference in the world, and coaching has become one of the most rewarding things you have ever done. Except when you suddenly feel like you just got punched in the face.

By a 6-year-old.

Wait... did you not see that punch coming? Because I did... and I'm *way over here.*

Your inner 6-year-old, if she's anything like mine, is actually a highly skilled pugilist, capable of delivering knockout blows that can bring us to our knees—it's her way of trying to get your attention.

Holy mother of cheese and crackers, *what is hap-pen-ning?*

Welcome to *The Land of WTF,* Coach. It's where we all go when life throws us a curve ball, also known as an AFGO: *Another Freakin' Growth Opportunity,* and starting your own business is riddled with AFGOs. They'll either make you buckle at the knees (if your inner 6-year-old is in the driver's seat of your life) or they'll grow you up, but only if your Adult

Self takes the wheel. It's your responsibility to know when to call your Adult Self into action—she's the one that needs to be in the driver's seat when it comes to doing grown up stuff—like running a business! The bad news is that we usually can't tell who's driving, and we often leave our inner 6-year-old in charge of adult responsibilities.

Starting your own business is a job for the *woman* in you—the one who knows a thing or two about how to take charge, how to get what she wants, how to fight for what matters to her. Yeah, *that* woman; that's who we need to show up for this party because she knows that no matter how tough it gets, she has the ability to figure things out.

There's a big difference between having a coaching *practice* and running a coaching *business*. Life coach training doesn't prepare you for the business side of coaching. That's what this book is about: everything you need to know about turning your practice into a business, and not just any business—it's got to be the kind of business that fills your soul *and* make you money.

As women we're often told that we have to put ourselves first, and I think that's difficult for us to hear. We think it means we have to push our loved ones out of the way so we can selfishly put ourselves at the top of our to-do list. So I'd like to clarify what it really means, because it certainly does *not* mean you love your children less, or your spouse, or anyone else for that matter. It means that you love them so much you want to show up with a big heart and arms wide open—the best you can be. Putting yourself first means that your number one priority is to clean up the mental clutter in your mind, because, let's face it, how much fun are you when you're bursting at the seams with resentment, exhaustion, and overwhelm?

This book is about both the business of being a life coach and the mindset you need to have in order to take the kind of action necessary to build a successful business, no matter how you may choose to define success. There are no false promises made in this book. Ultimately, you're the only one who gets to decide whether your business sizzles, or fizzles. But I can promise you this: when you grow up and into your role as a gutsy glorious business woman, your whole life will change.

There is no "easy" road to success and you know that. You also know that when you're in the right frame of mind—when your Adult Self is in charge of your life—everything seems easier, no matter how much energy you put into it.

Let's put that 6-year-old safely in the backseat. This is woman's work.

Business just got real, Coach.

Lin E.

1

MINDSET

B race yourself—Your inner Business Woman is about to be set free. But it's going to take some serious *guts* on your part to make that happen. Lots of guts. A veritable profusion of guts. Why? Because you'll be going up against your inner 6-year-old. Do not underestimate her— she thinks she's in charge of your life.

Are you ready to take the leap?

And, just to be clear, I'm not talking about some quantum leap here. A quantum leap occurs when a subatomic particle (no, not a human) goes from point A to point B *without passing through any of the points between A and B.*

LIN M. ELEOFF

Unless you're a subatomic particle (you're not, are you?) you cannot make a quantum leap from life coaching practice to life coaching business because it's just not possible to travel through space and time without visiting all the points in between. Those "points in between" are all the steps you need to take (46 in all!) in order to get your business up and running in a way that will be both fulfilling *and* income-generating. In other words, it's not enough to throw up a website and call it a business.

You'll know you're trying to take a quantum leap when you say things like, *"I shouldn't have to do all this,"* and, *"This shouldn't be so hard."*

Let me be very clear, because the last thing you want is for someone else to pull the wool over your lovely eyes: This *is* hard. Your job is to not make it feel harder than it actually is. After all, this isn't anything you can't handle. But the actual degree of "hard" in this work is going to depend entirely on how hard you keep telling yourself it is!

Besides, your business is an AFGO.[1] It's just another opportunity for you to grow up and into your life. If you let it, your business will reveal to you all the places where you still feel "exposed." That's the *best* thing about becoming a

---

[1] AFGO = Another *Freakin'* Growth Opportunity

business woman: it's yet another chance for you to meet your Self. To embrace the glory that is in you. That woman? Hard things are not enough to deter her. Overwhelm doesn't overcome her. And the Land of WTF is a place in her rear-view mirror.

౭౧

A newly-minted life coach recently sent me an email inquiring as to how I might be able to help her "figure out a few things," most notably... "how to get clients." Her email went on to say...

> *"It's embarrassing to admit this, but I really believed that once I finished my coach training, all I'd have to do was put up a website, start blogging, promote my blog posts on Facebook, which people would read and start sharing, and that would make everyone want to sign up to coach with me."*

And then there was this private message I received from a fellow coach:

> *"Hey Lin, there's something on my mind and I hope you don't mind if I ask you this: Am I the only coach out there who can't seem to make a living at this? I mean, I've been at it for a year and I can't seem to get*

3

any traction. I have a website and I blog every week. I have one or two clients but that's not enough to make me quit my day job. I'm starting to worry there's something wrong with me. My confidence has disappeared."

Sadly, messages like these are not uncommon but I've set out on a mission to eradicate them.

I know you've got the life experience. I know you've got the desire. I know you're a good coach. Now it's time to harness that inner Business Woman in you. The one with all the guts.

Let the glory-seeking begin.

Your First Business Trip

Pack your bags. You're about to go on your first business trip. Get ready because it's going to be a bumpy ride at first, fraught with Binary Hexadecimal Numbers, HyperText Markup Language, and File Transfer Protocols. (Not to mention Intellectual Property law, DMCA Takedowns, and SERPs.)

Unfortunately there are no direct flights. In fact, there will be four stops, each coinciding with the four psychological stages of competency. What a coincidence! The four stages for learning any new skill was a model introduced by Noel Burch in the 1970s. It describes the psychological states of mind involved in transforming one's *incompetence* in a particular skill to *competence* or even outright *mastery*.

This is a business trip like no other, I'll guarantee you that. You and your business are going to go through a metamorphosis together. This isn't just about learning the "mechanics" of building a business (that's all in part 2 of this book), it's also about shifting your mindset, from life coach to business woman. You really can't have a thriving business that makes you want to sing when you get up in the morning— excited to go to "work" every day—without understanding that it is indeed a test of your *emotional intelligence* as well as your ability to master new skills.

Do you have a tendency towards motion-sickness? Because there's no magic pill for the turbulence that's coming your way. The only thing you have control over is how you will choose to respond when the turbulence hits.

Brace yourself.

THE FOUR STAGES OF (BUSINESS) COMPETENCY

Stage One—Unconscious Incompetence: You have no idea what you don't know and you haven't a clue where to begin... everything's a blur. Nobody actually likes being in Stage One, understandably, because this is where Self Doubt likes to hang out. But pretending to be ready to move on is futile. Denial runs rampant in Stage One and it's so hard to spot denial when we are hip-deep in it. In Stage One, we tend to believe *everything* our mind tells us, even when it doesn't make logical sense. Overwhelm and procrastination are symptoms of the Stage One mindset, where we like to to say things like, "I'm try-*inggggggg*" a lot, as if trying is all that's required of us. Stage One feels a lot like The Land of WTF.

Stage Two—Conscious Incompetence: You're becoming aware that you've got some mind-shifting to do. You can see the flaws in your thinking, and in the underlying belief systems that leave you feeling inadequate and "less than" your fellow coaches. You're thinking that maybe, just *maybe*, you might we willing to slow down a bit to work these out, but then overwhelm seeps back in. You tend to shift from feeling hopeful to hopeless and helpless at any given moment. You'll know you're in Stage Two when you start to get really good at AFGO spotting—seeing the growth opportunity in the obstacle; it's just that you're not sure you can handle the obstacle... yet. Learning to trust that you'll be able to figure it all out is the gentle leap you're going for in Stage Two, which is really all about surrendering to what *is*. Whatever "it" is that's not working, or hasn't happened yet, you're learning to accept it. You realize that, although it's hard to build a business, that doesn't mean it's impossible.

Stage Three—Conscious Competence: Whoa! You have moments where you feel like you're in *the zone*, and you've got the mindset to prove it. You're learning how to do new things, even though it may still take a lot of effort on your part. You can practically feel yourself growing up. One of the biggest things you've learned is how to give Self Doubt a quick kick in the backside as soon as it shows up. Conscious competence is like riding a bike with both hands on the handlebars, but feeling confident enough to take one hand off to wave at someone or scratch your nose. You still have to concentrate, but you have moments where you feel like you can do things with your eyes closed. Business feels *good* in Stage Three.

Stage Four—Unconscious Competence: This is where we all want to be, right? Riding our bikes with our hands up in the air. Unconscious competence is when you're able to do

something competently *without even having to think about it.*
You rarely second-guess yourself in Stage Four. You're also
not afraid to try new things, even if that means going back to
Stage One. In Stage Four you're doing business *at the speed of
badass* and The Land of WTF is miles back, no longer even
visible in your rear-view mirror.

To be sure, moving through each of these four stages of
competency will be made easier (or more difficult), depending
on your ability to handle the turbulence—the emotional
aspect—that accompanies learning a new skill. Your goal isn't to
find a way to Stage Four and never leave, but to have the
emotional intelligence to know that the tide will ebb and flow
and there will be times when you may even find yourself back
in Stage One, which is likely to happen as you move through
the mechanics of running a business in Part Two. Your
ultimate goal is strive for a state of *unconscious competence* in
anything you take on, so that you're running your coaching
business in a gutsy and soulful way, with tried and true systems
in place that allow you to experience the freedom you signed
up for when you became a business woman in the first place.

By the way, this isn't a straight-line journey—be prepared to get
bounced around, from unconsciousness to consciousness, and
then back again. It happens to all of us. But you already know

that it's never "one and done," right, Coach? The road goes on for as long as you've got places to go.

Who's The Boss?

You are of two minds: one is a frightened, petulant (yet utterly adorable) 6-year-old child, and the other is the mind of a gutsy, badass, card-carrying adult.

Which one is running your business?

It's not always easy to tell who's in the driver's seat of your life. Too often we unwittingly leave our mind on its default setting of "child" and, as you can imagine, that's going to mess you up whenever you're required to do adult tasks and solve adult problems that become emotional triggers for your inner 6-year-old.

Your **Child Mind** represents the part of you that learned to think about the world—and your place in it—long before she was even capable of making sense of it all. Your early life experiences shaped your Child Mind's worldview, and as you know, changing your worldview once you're an adult is a tricky thing. Old think-feel-do habits die hard. That's why, whenever an AFGO smacks you upside the head, your Child Mind reacts like a kid in a candy store without any money.

Allowing your Child Mind to remain in charge of any aspect of your life is like continuing to use a very old and outdated operating system and then wondering why things "always" go wrong. And yes, even coaches who realize they're eligible for an upgrade, often hang on to their ingrained think-feel-do habits whenever an AFGO smacks them upside the head. Like I always say, your business is an AFGO of epic proportions— just another opportunity to test your emotional intelligence.

Needless to say, there are a lot of bugs and missing features in the old operating system and when you keep using that system, your business will be run accordingly—from the point of view of a child who simply hasn't got the chops to be running a business, let alone your adult life. Is it any wonder that she messes up when she's allowed to remain in charge?

By the way, if you're not sure what your Child Mind sounds like, it's usually something like this:

> *This is wayyyyyyy too hard.*

> *I don't wanna do this stuff.*

> *Nobody likes me.*

> *I'm not good enough for this.*

> *I'm stupid.*

I can't do it like she does.

Gimme a cookie!

Without awareness of our Child Mind's antics, we continue to wait for someone else to rush in and solve our problems; to fix things; to make it all better.

I realize I'm preaching to the choir here, Coach, but it's too easy (and unwise) to ever think we've got our Child Mind all figured out and that we know how to deal with her. And it would be a mistake to simply try to push her aside and "take charge." Your inner 6-year-old doesn't need to be "figured out." She just needs **Adult Mind** to slip into the driver's seat so she can hop on over to the passenger side and stick her head out the window and let the wind blow on her face. She's part of the intricate fabric of who we are as women, and she needs our love more than anything.

Your Adult Mind is the part of you that's capable of higher level *thinking,* thanks to a fully-developed prefrontal cortex— the part of the brain that's responsible for your ability to think logically and reasonably, to be discerning, to use your judgement, and to solve problems, like the kinds of problems we face when we start a business; the kinds of problems that make our Child Mind want to run for the hills.

If you're not sure what your Adult Mind sounds like, it's usually something like this:

> *I've got this.*

> *I can figure this out.*

> *This is exciting.*

> *This is hard but that's expected.*

> *I'm going to give this my absolute best shot.*

And this is what she says to the child in her that's been hoping and praying for someone to step in an take care of her:

> *Don't worry, darling, I've got the wheel. I'll give it back to you when it's time for us to play!*

Ever notice those times in your life when you feel unstoppable? On fire. In control.

And utterly badass.

That's when you know you were using the upgraded operating system, even if by accident. Draw on that experience to inform you what it feels like to be using your Adult Mind. You know that feeling—you can get a lot of things done when you step up and into your adult life.

Your Child Mind, with her limited capacity to make sense of the world, let alone your business, also has a "feeling." Learn to spot it: it often feels like shame, or vulnerability, or helplessness. And that's how you'll know you've got an AFGO on your hands.

The reason we get stuck in our businesses (among other things in life) is that we haven't fully reconciled Child Mind with Adult Mind.

And reconcile, we must.

℘

If you've been trying to build your coaching business for a while and can't seem to get anywhere, it may be that you're recycling the same old thoughts using the outdated software your Child Mind wants to hold onto because that's what it knows best. It's like washing your clothes in dirty water—you may even be able to clean up some of those thoughts, but, as in a raucous game of Whac-a-Mole, they pop right back up again. And again (and again).

While your brain may be capable of deciphering, decoding, calculating, innovating, and even meta-cogitating, there will come a time when you need to tune in to the intelligence and wisdom of your heart. Your heart is the real Boss of your business. Your heart is not capable of steering you wrong when it comes to creating a business you love and that you're proud of. Even though Adult Mind can bring logic and reasoning to the table, your heart brings a deeper sense of intuitive "knowing" to the mix.

After all, this isn't just business, Coach. This is deeply personal.

When you rush in to take action to grow your business, without understanding who's the boss, you'll only be able to get so far. And then you'll feel stuck. We often get the brilliant idea to use fear to motivate us, to talk ourselves into things, and then out of things, and to trick ourselves into believing that we have no options. Most of us were well trained to do exactly this, whether by our parents, in school, our relationships, or in our first jobs. It's a kind of low-level management, but it works—to a point.

Whenever you find Child Mind back in the driver's seat (having one of her tell-tale hissy fits, or making you feel ashamed or vulnerable), the last thing you need is to "motivate" yourself into taking action from a place of fear. Please slow down and listen here, because this might be the opposite of what you've done in the past. Bypassing the AFGO and using brute force to push through an obstacle will only make Child Mind panic and turn on you, hauling out the F-word (failure!!) and telling you to just give it up.

Don't fall for it, Coach.

Your Child Mind may be paralyzed by the AFGO that your business has smacked you with but your Adult Mind knows better because it's more in tune with your heart. Use it to remind yourself that you know what to do, and when you don't, you have the ability to figure it out.

Why You Can't Do This Without Dignity

Having the guts to start a business requires more than determination, daring, and grit. You also need **dignity,** which can only come with the deep knowing that you are worthy of all the love in the world, you are enough—just the way you are—and you matter, simply because you were born.

When you have the guts to believe you are worthy of building a successful business, you will build a successful business. When you have the guts to accept that you are enough, just the way you are, you will become a business woman, if that's what you want to do with your "enough-ness." And when you have the guts to boldly claim your place in the world, because you

know how much you matter—simply because you are here—
then anything you offer to the world also matters.

It's not enough to get this in your head—you've got to feel the
powerful and unmistakeable energy shift that occurs when you
grasp this with your heart. There's a formidable inner strength
that comes when you reclaim your dignity. You can tell
whether someone's got it or not by the way they live their lives,
and on whose terms.

You were born with dignity. As a baby you didn't think twice
about making sure you got what you needed, no matter if it
inconvenienced anyone else. Actually, as a baby, you weren't
even able to think. But as you got older you learned to
(mistakenly) think that maybe you weren't the hot stuff you
once believed you were. Goodbye dignity.

It's virtually a rite of passage: we are born with Dignity, we
invariably lose it thanks to self doubt, then we have to fight like
hell to get it back. It's kind of like losing our baby teeth, except
that having another set of teeth grow back is inevitable.
Reclaiming our dignity is entirely optional. It takes some real
guts on our part to get it back.

80

You've probably been able to reclaim your dignity at certain times in your life, only to lose it again. Can you see how it was in those rare moments when you had such clarity about yourself that you were able to stand up so tall you could practically feel your roots take hold as you simultaneously reached up for the sky to grasp your heart's desire? That's the feeling *we all want*. That's really the only feeling we've *ever* wanted.

So dignified.

To the extent that we, as coaches-who-want-to-be-business-women, are able to dissolve all the old beliefs that make us feel unworthy of business success; or ashamed that we're not good enough, or that our coaching services don't really matter that much—all these feelings are tell-tale signs that we have to get our dignity back, and that takes all the guts you can muster if you want to experience the glory that comes with being a woman who is authentic to her core and unapologetic for going after her dreams.

The purpose here isn't to become the world's best life coach or to build a big fat business. This is about believing in yourself so fully and completely that becoming a really good coach or building a highly successful business is merely a *natural consequence* of having had the guts to go for it all.

17

That's what dignity gets you.

Extreme Self Coaching

Get ready to start coaching yourself in the *extreme*. Of course, this is optional, but I have a feeling you're ready for a deeper dive. Besides, starting your own business is bound to bring up your shiitakes, big time, along with those familiar feelings that go hand in hand with self doubt.

Extreme Self Coaching (ESC) demands more of you—an even closer look into how well you really know and understand your *Self.* How will you choose to "package" yourself for business? What do you want the world to see? What do you want to keep hidden? Do you have the guts to take your rightful place on the life coaching stage?

ESC is a process of becoming vigilant when it comes to who's The Real Boss of your business in any given moment. It will help you take thought work to a whole new level of *deep.*

If you're familiar with *metacognition,* you know that it's what sets humans apart from the animal world; it's our ability to *think about what we're thinking about* that makes us unique as a species. It's a *Homo sapiens* thing.

Coaches, I find, are more willing to take metacognition up a notch. It's what I love most about working with my coach clients: not only do we speak the same language but we're both aware that we can always go deeper.

It takes guts to relentlessly pursue the thoughts and beliefs that are like poison pills that make us feel some version of "less than" and then dismantle them one-by-one, so that all that's left is you—without the drama, without the excuses, without the self doubt.

ESC is about excising, with surgical precision, the thoughts that sound good (logical, magnanimous, sincere) but are *actually not good* for you, such as:

I'm trying as best I can.

I already did that.

I already know that.

I can't figure this out.

There must be something missing.

It's not my fault.

Maybe I'm just not cut out for this.

I've got so much to do.

I've got more important things to do.

That last one? If it's really true, then you need to honor those other "more important" things and stop dabbling in business building. You really can't be "a little bit business woman" and expect a lot of results. This only serves to set yourself up for failure and gives you more evidence (conveniently so) that it's all just "too hard."

�

Building a business is an inside job as much as it appears to be an outside one—and more. On the inside it requires grit, grace, and the guts to be willing to coach yourself in the extreme. Think of *Extreme* Self Coaching as mindfulness on steroids. And yes, at times it will feel like you're playing an endless game of "Whac-a-Mole," because just when you think you've got it, *you've really got it*, another AFGO will come along and slap the other side of your head. And if you're not paying attention, if you've allowed your mind to return to its default setting of "child," then don't be so surprised when you come undone.

On the outside, our business is loaded with learning new skills, which often sends us straight to The Land of WTF, that place where all hell breaks loose and we have no clue how much we don't know about what we think we know a lot about. (Wait. *What?*)

Listen up, Coach, it's not about the obstacle; it's *never* about the obstacle. It's about how you choose to perceive the obstacle and your subsequent response to it. Following is an example of how to coach yourself in the *extreme* whenever an obstacle threatens to get the best of you.

> **Step 1:** Say hello to the obstacle—you knew it would arrive at some point.

> **Step 2:** Identify your state of mind: are you in Child Mind or Adult Mind?

> **Step 3:** Metacogitate, i.e., detach from your mind so as to observe your reaction to the obstacle. What do you notice about yourself from this point of view? (Stay with Step 3 until you are able to shift into Adult Mind, no matter how long it takes.)

> **Step 4:** With Adult Mind in charge, make a decision about how you're going to handle the obstacle in a way that is actually helpful to you and useful for your business.

> **Step 5:** Identify the lesson learned—how did you manage to grow yourself up, thanks to the obstacle?

Example: Obstacle = Your computer crashes

> **Step 1:** Hello obstacle. I hate you.

> **Step 2:** Child Mind

> **Step 3:** *"I'm having a hissy fit and want to break things."* And eventually, *"Ok, this is pointless, I'll never figure out what to do when I'm indulging my Child Mind."*

> **Step 4:** Adult Mind decides to call Bob—he'll be able to help out right away.

> **Step 5:** *"I see how much I indulge my Child Mind by allowing it to spend time in the drama of it all and how much less energy it takes when I ditch the drama and simply figure out how to solve the problem."*

When you resolve to *expect* the obstacles that invariably come with starting your own business, you're much more prepared to diffuse any ensuing drama. You don't have to slay the obstacles so much as understand *why each one is an obstacle for you.* What is the obstacle *really* about? Because, at first, it may look as though it's about the obstacle. Look again.

Yes, your computer will crash. Your website will get shut down. Someone will probably demand a refund after taking one of your programs. They'll question your professionalism. Things will go wrong and your *emotional buttons* will get pushed, causing your Child Mind to throw a fit. What will you do next? Hopefully, you'll say, "Hello, obstacle," then follow the rest of the ESC process until you come up with a grown up answer that will solve the problem.

Get Off The Fence, Coach!

This is where I take my clients aside so we can have The Talk.

This is where I tell them they have to pick a side and stop straddling the fence.

This is where the shiitakes invariably hit the fan, if they don't GET OFF THE FENCE!

Are you *all in*, or are you a little bit in and a little bit out? Remember, you can't be "a little bit business woman" *unless* you're perfectly happy *dabbling* in entrepreneurship. If that's the case, I support you fully and completely, but you still can't stay on the fence. Own the fact that you want to dabble—no one says you can't—and accept the awesome results that dabbling also brings.

Either way, you must get down off the fence. I know you can come up with all kinds of reasons for staying up there, but fence sitting is just another way to avoid the AFGO. And why would you do that? Probably because your mind is telling you that you don't have the guts to pull this off. Your mind is focusing on the obstacles. And what did we learn about obstacles in the last chapter?

Repeat after me: *It's never about the obstacle.* It's about how you perceive the obstacle and how you use it to keep yourself perched on the fence OR to grow yourself up.

I get it, it feels nice and safe up there on the fence. You don't have to worry about disappointing anyone if you don't give them anything to be disappointed about. You don't have to be afraid of what people will think of your website and your blog if you don't put it all out there. You don't have to fight for what you want if you tell yourself it's "their fault" you can't have it, and that you've "tried everything" but none of it worked.

Nice try, Coach. That's just your Child Mind trying to fake you out, again. Don't fall for it.

Get off the fence, Coach.

I'll admit, I've had my share of fence sitting. I've managed to talk myself down from the fence on several occasions. Yes, it was hard. At times, it was really *really* hard, I'll give you that. The thing about the fence is that you think you've got a pretty good view of how things ought to be. The truth is, you have no idea what might happen if you decided to jump off and go all in. The view is much better down here, on ground level, where you can get a clear perspective of what's tripping you up and what you need to do to fix it.

Pick a side, Coach.

Ignore your mind's penchant for saying things like, "I don't know," and to hedge, hem, haw and deny your heart's desire.

The truth is, you do know.

And if you really don't know? Well, make it your business to find out. Either way, don't fall for the head fake, the way your Child Mind uses "I don't know" as a way to allow you to stay up there on the fence.

> *I don't know what to name my business.*

> *I don't know who my "avatar" is.*

> *I don't know what colors to pick.*

> *I don't know what niche to target.*

> *I don't know what theme I want for my website.*

> *I don't know how to "sell" myself.*

> *I don't know how much to charge.*

I don't know if anyone will like this.

I don't know what to write about.

I don't know what to call myself.

I don't know what to put in my sandwich.

Every reason you give yourself for staying on the fence is like taking a tiny drop of poison. It doesn't taste like poison, mind you; it actually tastes pretty good, makes you think you don't have to get down off that fence. That's the worst kind of poison, the kind you think is actually good for you.

And if you're really struggling up there on the fence and can't seem to coach yourself down, I encourage you to speak to a coach who can help. Also, consider joining my private coaching group on Facebook by going to **gutsyglorious.com** and asking to join. There's an amazing group of women in that group and they're always available to help a fellow coach out.

Do You Really Have the Guts for This?

Being a business owner is not for the faint of heart. You've got to be sure you're up to the challenge because it *will* challenge you.

Whether you like to call yourself an entrepreneur or a business woman, soulpreneur or lady-boss, what matters is that you understand what you are committing yourself to.

Answer the following questions truthfully... no one is going to see your answers. I realize you may not have some of the answers—that's what Part 2 of this book is for. I just want to give you a clear picture of the road that lies ahead, and the topics we will cover.

1. Why do you want to have your own business as opposed to working for someone else?

2. What is it about your character that lends itself to being an entrepreneur as opposed to an employee?

3. How much time (daily, weekly, monthly) are you able and willing to spend on your business?

4. How much can you afford to invest in start-up costs?

5. Have you identified a target market you'd like to serve?

6. What sorts of products and services will you offer?

7. How long will it take you to create these products and services?

8. Who is your competition? Whose work do you admire, whose work has influenced you, and how can you put a new spin on your work to create a brand?

9. How will you cover your "assets" online? Are you aware of what it will take to protect your personal and family assets?

10. What legal structure will you choose for your business?

11. Do you have a strategy for how to get your business up and running?

12. Are you excited to do this?

I had no idea what launching an online business would entail and I might've passed over questions like the ones I posed to you above, thinking, "It'll be fine. I'll figure it out." But I have to admit, there were many times when it wasn't fine, where I felt like throwing in the towel, and I realize it's because I didn't spend some time up front to really understand the nature of the undertaking and appreciate how much resolve and resilience starting your own business requires.

So, never again can you simply say, "I had no idea." Because, yes, I guess I did tell you so.

When you're finally ready to get off the fence and move on to the action steps of building your business, I've got a contract for you to sign (I can't help it—I'm a lawyer). It may very well be the most important contract you ever attach your signature to, so be sure to practice due diligence and really examine your intentions before signing!

LIN M. ELEOFF

AGREEMENT BETWEEN ME AND MY INNER BUSINESS WOMAN

I, _____, hereby enter into this binding agreement with my **Inner Business Woman**, freely and willingly and without duress, and in consideration for all the love and respect we have for each other.

I intend to honor the terms of this agreement fully and make the following promise:

1.   To keep my guts about me; and to follow the *Extreme* Self Coaching process whenever I get smacked upside the head by an AFGO/obstacle.

2.   To follow each of the Action Steps outlined in Part Two of this book and to check things off one by one until they're all done.

3.   To block off time in my calendar each day, Monday through Friday, to do the work as outlined throughout this book, whether it's *Extreme* Self Coaching or the Action Steps.

4.   To not make excuses such as, "I don't have time," "I don't know how," and, "This is too hard."

5.   To treat my business with respect.

6.   To treat my Self with respect.

7.   To not be afraid of failure.

8.   To do whatever it takes to succeed.

9.   To not care about what They think.

10. To trust my own opinion.

11. To never apologize for the Coach, Boss, Woman I am becoming.

12. To get off the fence.

_____   _____
Signed   Date

30

2

ACTION

Y ou are now entering The Action Zone *Zone Zone Zone Zone.*

The Land of WTF is in your rear-view mirror! (But only temporarily. You get that, right?)

Your sleeves are rolled up. Best of all, you're ready to *show up and do your work,* no matter what.

No matter if something doesn't work... you'll find a way to fix it.

No matter if someone doesn't like what you're doing... it's what *you* think is best for you and your business that counts.

You're going to build your business on rock—not sand—and you're going to put a virtual electric fence around it. Your business is your baby, after all, and you need to protect it.

All. Damn. Day.

Every. Day.

Right?

You know ahead of time that when you lose your footing, start to waffle or otherwise start backing into The Land of WTF (that swirly place where Self Doubt seems to grab you by the throat and slam you against the wall), you know it's time to go back into Thought Rehab, so you can clean up the mess your Child Mind has been allowed to make (bless her endearing, trouble-making heart). You'll then stand up straight and tall, muster up your not-so-secret stash of guts, and get back *out there*, where you *belong*.

The best part? You are looking at what's ahead of you now, with both eyes wide open. You know there will be more AFGOs that come knocking, testing your Heart's desire to become a badass-to-the-bone business owner in your own right. You also understand exactly what is required of you at all times: to do your absolute best work, no matter what They think.

You're not worried anymore that you don't know how to do things because you are rock solid in your belief that *you have the ability to figure out how to do things you don't yet know how to do.*

You're ready to start taking action on a daily basis to build a business that will make you money, and will also make you happy, however you may choose to define happiness in your life. Whether it's walking through a park without worrying about paying the bills, or walking in your sky-high Jimmy Choos without having to justify how you spend your money, you have a plan and a fire under your tail to get you there.

You've got guts to spare, and share. In fact, you've got more guts than you ever realized... way more than your Child Mind ever allowed you to believe. You know what you stand for and you're ready to stand up for it.

You're going to build your online platform—your website, your blog and/or your podcast, and your programs and services—and then offer it all to the world.

You're ready to be BOSS. And saying things to yourself like, "I'll do it tomorrow," never goes unchallenged, because you're on to the wily tricks of your Child Mind.
You've got guts and *you know it.*

LIN M. ELEOFF

THE PROCESS OF TAKING ACTION

This is the part where you start building your business step by step. There are 46 of them in all.

Follow the bouncing ball and, when you're done, you'll have a business.

A soulful, money-making business.

One that rocks your sexy socks off.

We're going to cover it all. I want to give you a big-picture overview of what you simply *must do* to launch, grow, and protect your online coaching business. I understand you may look at the steps and realize you've already done some of them. Please read over that section anyway. You may pick up on something new, or a way to make what you've already done even better, or at least be able to breathe a sigh of relief that you're further along than you may have realized.

Also, there's a method to the order of the steps and I've arranged them this way for the coach who is either starting from scratch, or has been coaching for a while yet her business isn't progressing the way she'd like it to.

The 46 Steps are meant to build on each other. For example, there's no point in registering your business name if you don't

34

have a clear idea what your target market or ideal client profile looks like. This isn't to say you can't skip ahead or rearrange the order of the steps; by all means, do what works best for you. Just make sure that, in the end, you've placed a checkmark beside each of the 46 steps. I've created a downloadable checklist for you at GutsyGloriousLifeCoach.com. Be sure to print it out and keep it handy—it will keep you on track, on task, and focused.

Are you ready to start taking action? Remember to keep tabs on what your minds are doing—and make sure Child Mind isn't in the driver's seat. Keep tabs on your attitude as you do this work, checking in with yourself whenever you feel overwhelmed, stuck, or find yourself drifting off to another project. If you have to, take a moment to get back in to your Adult Mind so that you can give your gutsy glorious business the attention it so rightly deserves.

Your business is your baby. You need to protect it. But you also need to love it. Deeply. And since love is both a verb and a feeling, you'll need to get your Adult Mind on board in order to feel and do your business in a love-ly way.

Ready? Action!

STEP 1: ESTIMATE YOUR COSTS

When you're just starting a business you've got to have some idea how much it's going to cost so you can budget accordingly.

Keep in mind that your expenses will change as your business grows, but it is possible to start your online business without investing a lot of money in the beginning. Time, however, is another story—you're going to have to invest a lot of that.

Of course, if you're working from home, like most coaches, you won't have the added expense of renting an office.

Following is a run-down of the basic start-up costs you can expect, some of which are one-time investments, others will be ongoing operational expense. If you're careful, you can keep your initial investment quite low (depending on whether you need to purchase a computer or laptop).

- Computer or Laptop + Monthly Internet Service

- Cell Phone + Monthly Cell Phone Service

- Business Registration/Filing Fees

- Domain Name Registration (Yearly)

- Web Hosting Fees, i.e., where your website will live (as low as $3.95 a month)

- Website Theme (although Wordpress does offer some free themes)

- Website Design (you can spend a few hundred dollars or thousands)

- Email List Management Service/Autoresponder software (Monthly)

- Shopping Cart/Payment System (monthly + percentage)

As I mentioned, money isn't the only thing you'll be investing in your business. You must also calculate how much *time* you'll have to spend on getting your business up and running. Don't be surprised if it turns out to be a lot more than you expected. Your job is to carve out the amount of time you can afford to dedicate to working on your business without feeling guilty, and without having to apologize to anyone because you're doing something you love.

STEP 2: KNOW THE LAW

There's actually no such thing as "Internet Law," at least not in the same way we have defined areas such as contract law, criminal law, constitutional law, etc. Instead, what we have is an interpretation of pre-existing intellectual property laws, as well as consumer protection laws, all of which have been applied to new legal issues that have arisen since the dawn of the digital age. It's safe to say that Internet law remains in a state of flux and that new technology continues to raise new policy questions regarding online business best practices.

For the most part, businesses in the United States are governed by state laws. That means the law may be different from state to state, and you'd be wise not to assume that what's allowed in California is also true for Massachusetts. Each state has the power to create its own set of laws concerning the formation and operation of businesses within its borders. That said, the *United States Uniform Law Commission* and the *National Conference of State Legislatures* are responsible for creating consistency across most states. However, no law is effective in any particular state unless its legislature formally adopts it.

This is where YOU come in.

You must **practice due diligence** and make it your business to understand the business laws of your state and local governments as well as any applicable federal laws. There are also local government laws, bylaws and ordinances you must become familiar with in order to stay in compliance with the laws of your particular jurisdiction. Because you do not want to get fined or sued—or worse, be forced to wear one of those orange jumpsuits they make you wear in jail. Nobody (and I mean nobody) looks good in orange. Or a jumpsuit for that matter.

Below is an overview of the laws that are most likely to impact your coaching business.

Federal Law

The Federal Trade Commission (FTC)

The Federal Trade Commission is the primary government agency responsible for regulating e-commerce activities.

The role of the FTC is twofold: to protect consumers from unfair and deceptive business practices, and to prevent unfair methods of competition in commerce. That means the FTC is on both your side, as well as that of the consumer. To the extent that you are doing business directly with consumers, then you'd best pay attention to the rules and regulations that affect the use of commercial emails, internet advertising, online sales and marketing, testimonials and endorsements, the tracking of people's online behavior, personal data and contact information, consumer privacy, and more, a lot of which will be discussed in the coming chapters.

The Children's Online Privacy Protection Act (COPPA)

The Children's Online Privacy Protection Act regulates the collection of personal information from children under the age of 13 on the Internet. Specifically, COPPA applies to personally identifiable information (PII) that is collected from children online, such as their full name, home address, email address, telephone number, or any other type of information that would allow someone to identify the child or contact the child. Website operators must post a privacy policy that is prominently displayed and which discloses whether the site collects PII from children under 13, and if so, the exact nature of the information collected and how that information will be used. Furthermore, any website that collects PII from a child under the age of 13 must first obtain "verifiable parental consent" from that child's parent or guardian.

A website operator must also give a parent the option to agree to the collection and use of the child's PII without agreeing to the disclosure of the information to third parties.

The United States Patent and Trademark office (USPTO)

The USPTO is the federal agency responsible for granting patents and federally registering trademarks in the United States. Its mandate is to promote the progress of science and the useful arts, and to protect the rights of authors and inventors to choose how, when, and where their works may be used or displayed by others.

The United States Copyright Act, Title 17

The United States Copyright Act was created to, in effect, protect original works of authorship, or "writings." These days, the word writings has come to include architectural design, software, graphic arts, motion pictures, and sound recordings. Regardless, if a work has been fixed in a tangible medium of expression, it is protected by Title 17. Copyright registration is done through the U.S. Copyright Office.

LIN M. ELEOFF

The Digital Millennium Copyright Act (DMCA)

The Digital Millennium Copyright Act was enacted in 1998,
and it made major changes to the U.S. Copyright Act. It
brought U.S. copyright law into compliance with the *World
Intellectual Property Organization (WIPO) Copyright Treaty*
and the *WIPO Performances Phonograms Treaty.* The
DMCA also strengthened the legal protection of intellectual
property rights following the advent of the Internet. A DMCA
"Takedown" occurs when notice is given that copyrighted
content is being displayed on a website without authorization.
The DMCA Takedown is an order issued to the Online
Service Provider to remove the unauthorized content from a
website on its server at the request of the rightful owner of the
copyright.

Controlling the Assault of Non-Solicited Pornography and Marketing Act
(CAN-SPAM Act)

The Can Spam Act regulates the use of commercial email,
establishes requirements for commercial messages, gives email
recipients the right to have a sender stop emailing them, and
calls for swift and painful penalties for violations of the Act. It
allows courts to set damages of up to USD $2 million when

spammers break the law. Federal district courts are even allowed to send spammers to jail and/or award punitive damages if the violation is determined to be willful.

Intellectual Property Law

Intellectual property (IP) is lawyer-speak for the brilliance that comes out of your mind.

This legal term refers to ideas that exist in tangible form (because an idea alone cannot be protected). IP is a property right that can be protected by federal and state law. Such protection gives exclusive rights as to how a creation or work is used. These rights are granted for a certain period of time, depending on the type of IP.

The Internet Corporation for Assigned Names and Numbers (ICANN)

ICANN (ICANN.org) is a non-profit public-benefit organization run by people from all over the world who are committed to keeping the Internet safe, stable, and as secure as possible. It is a policy-making body that has great influence over how countries create rules and regulations concerning the

Internet, as well as a unique role in its infrastructure. It has contracts with registries (such as dot-com or dot-info) and registrars (companies that sell domain names to individuals) and that helps define how the domain name system (DNS) works around the world. ICANN is not a lawmaker, per se, but it does have tremendous influence over how the Internet evolves and expands around the globe.

Office of the Secretary of State (SOS)

Each state is responsible for regulating business activities that occur within its borders. In most states, that role falls under the *Office of the Secretary of State*, also called the *Secretary of the Commonwealth* or *Lieutenant Governor* in some states.

Be sure to familiarize yourself with the government office that regulates business in the state in which you live. You can find a lot of this information online, but make sure the government website has a ".gov" extension. That's where you will find information about the nuances of forming a business in your state, including corporate filing requirements.

Keep in mind, individual states typically have a wide range of rules and regulations that apply to companies doing business within their borders. Be sure to research the state-specific business laws that apply to your specific type of business, including laws for registering and/or incorporating a business. Once again, not all states have the same requirements, and it is not possible for this book to address all of the possibilities, so remember to practice due diligence and do your homework. Once you find the contact information for the governing body in your state, take note of it... you're going to need it again. And again.

Local Governments

Besides federal and state law, you must consider what other laws may affect your business at the local level. Most states have at least two more government tiers below them: Municipalities and Counties. These will govern through Municipal Laws, Bylaws, and Ordinances. Therefore you must also consider whether your county or municipality has rules, regulations, bylaws, or ordinances that may affect the way you do business, including what's allowed when it comes to setting up your home office. Be sure to research your local government's rules as they pertain to your business. And as I'm sure you know, ignorance is no excuse for breaking (or not complying with) the law.

STEP 3: WHO'S YOUR MAMA? OOPS, I MEAN...AVATAR!

Are you sick of the word "Avatar" yet? I thought I was, too. That was awhile back when I must've thought it would serve a purpose to think that way, but then I asked myself, "What's the point of that?" Did I need a new word to explain what this word so perfectly means? Did I really need to re-invent anything here? Same with "ideal client." Sometimes the lingo changes, but we're still talking about the same constructs.

I'd rather not try to fix what isn't broken. There's a lot of bull-hooey out there but the one about why you need to know your Avatar is not part of it.

Still, it's enough to make your head spin, isn't it? There's all that talk about demographics, psychographics, and even pretty graphics. You're supposed to "know your audience." You have to identify your "target market." You must be able to describe your "ideal client."

If you think I'm going to tell you that you don't have to worry about any of those things in this chapter, well, you will be disappointed. Take a stroll back into "Thought Rehab," and meet me back here once your head stops spinning, because we've got some serious work to do. Before we can figure out what your niche is (oh yeah, that's comin' too), we've got to figure out who you really REALLY *really* really rEAlly **really** want to work with. And figuring that out starts with you. Before we can identify your Avatar, we've got to know more about the people you like to hang out with. Because there's no sense in working with anyone who isn't a good fit for you. Don't apologize for that. There are coaches enough for everyone, and the right fit is a gift. When your clients are the kind of people you like to be around, then work doesn't feel like work.

Before we figure out what their problems are, let's determine what they're like.

- Describe the personality of someone you love to be around. We don't need to know their shoe size, for heaven's sake, but we do need to know who you want to hang out with.

- Next, what is it about *you* that makes you like being around people like that? Do you like hanging around people who like to laugh because you believe life shouldn't be taken too seriously? Then you most certainly don't want to attract people who take everything very seriously. That would make your days quite long!

- For fun, name three or four people you know whom you love hanging out with.

- Now, describe them in detail.

No, no, no, don't you skip this part. It's important.

Don't move on until you've nailed this description. You've got to be able to see that person in your mind. It doesn't matter what shoes she's wearing, or what she likes to eat, or the color of her hair. We just want to know what she is like. Take a moment. Write it down. I promise you: This is going to help everything you do going forward. While you're at it, give that new person a name. My Avatar's name is Carrie, because I picture her as being a lot like Carrie Bradshaw, in personality more so than style. (But I love it when one of my clients tells me she's really into handbags and shoes, like me!) I also imagine my avatar as being the gutsy risk-taking type who believes it's her role-model "duty" to get her ass to Happy while on the road to being Her Own Boss—which is why she's reading this book!

ACTION STEPS:

1. Identify 3 or 4 people you like to hang out with.

2. Describe, in detail, what they're like. (a.k.a. "psychographics.")

3. Flip through a magazine until you find a picture of someone whom you imagine looks just like the person you want to work with.

4. Give her a name.

5. Stick the picture up on your bathroom mirror.

6. Say "hello" to her every morning. Strike up conversations!

STEP 4: NICHE IT DOWN A.K.A. TARGET PRACTICE

Please don't roll your eyes when I say things like "target market." These phrases are just words that describe what we're talking about. Same goes for "unique selling proposition" and even the words "selling" and "marketing" themselves.

LIN M. ELEOFF

You may say you don't like these words. I caution you to not get caught up in semantics as an excuse to *avoid* taking action.

I was surprised when I recently read a fellow life coach's comments in a Facebook group where she said she "hated" terms like these because they sounded so "sales-y" and "business-y" and downright "sleazy." She couldn't see the harshness, nor the judgment, in her own words. I raise this here, not because she hurt my feelings (much), but because I couldn't help but wonder how she was hurting herself by getting wrapped up in such drama.

The shamanic teacher and healer Don Miguel Ruiz implores us to "be impeccable with [our] word," in his book, *The Four Agreements.* I take this to also mean that we must also be impeccable with the way we think, how we convey those thoughts out loud, and whether we're only serving to distract ourselves from the task at hand.

He also tells us not to "take anything personally," but I'll leave it at that.

Choosing a niche (along with your Avatar) is about *marketing.* It's about *how you talk to people* about their particular problem in a way that makes them want to listen to what you have to say.

If you don't know this about your particular Avatar—what keeps her up at night—then it will be very difficult for you to know what to write about, blog about, talk about, and *how* to write, blog, and talk about it. For example, if two people have the same problem--one of them is 25 and the other is 55—it will be very hard to market to both of them at the same time. Even with a similar problem, 25-year-olds think and talk differently than 55-year-olds and they will look for advice and influence from different places than those who are in their fifties; their life experience is totally different. Exactly who are you speaking to?

Choosing a niche is about speaking the language of your Avatar.

This is how you let her know that you understand what's bugging her. Which is why you simply have to "niche that baby down."

If you feel like throwing a shoe at me, that's fine. I'm used to it. My clients do the most moaning and groaning when I tell them they have to choose a niche. Some will even curl up into a ball and start reciting the nursery rhyme, *"Oh, do you know the muffin man, the muffin man, the muffin man...."*

But hear me on this: A coach without a niche is like Thelma without Louise, or Ben without Jerry (can you even imagine?) Why? Because when you know your niche—check that, when you *own* your niche—it says you understand exactly what a particular market "subset" needs, at least to the point where people start to think that you "get" them, you really *see* them. When people feel understood, heard, validated, and listened to, they will do whatever it takes to be around you, learn from you, grow with you, *hire* you, *pay* you to give them your inspired attention.

Choosing a niche is about talking in a way so your market will listen, and *listening* so your market will *talk*... to *you*.

You can't grow your business, at least not into one that's a real going concern, if you don't create a clear picture of who you're talking to. Our customers are much more than "targets," of course. On the contrary, they are often an inspiration to us, calling upon us to create deep and meaningful coaching products and services that your people are compelled to buy, not because of any slick marketing, but because they believe you're listening. Because you make them feel *heard.* Not to mention you're offering a solution that gives them hope.

Target Practice (wink!)

If you're trying to hone in on a niche, it's not enough to say that your target market is "women who feel stressed." First of all, I don't know many (any?) women who aren't feeling stressed at least some of the time. That's like a restaurant owner who says her target market is "hungry people." Can you imagine how many different dishes you would have to offer if you were trying to serve all hungry people? Burgers. Vegan fried rice. Meatballs. Matzo balls. Peanut butter sandwiches. Chicken nuggets. Lobster. Hot dogs. Steak. Falafels. Enchiladas. Succotash. Steak. Fries. Baba Ghanoush. Luo Han Zai. Ack!

Worse, after cooking all that food, chances are the only person who will show up is Nobody. How would Anybody who loves Baba Ganoush know about your delicious Baba Ganoush if your advertising says, "Good food. For hungry people. Try some." Have I made my point yet?

You digging what I'm saying?

∞

I've been working one-on-one with a client named Donna, who recently told me this story:

"Lin, I was at a party the other day, chatting with a man who asked me what I did for a living. Now, before working with you, I would say something like, "I'm a life coach and I help people who are in transition." This would usually make the other person's eyes glaze over until suddenly, they'd make a beeline for the hors d'oeuvres. But this time, I was ready—even though this man seemed like the last person I thought would be interested. I told him, "I'm an Empty Nest Life Coach." His response was, 'Oh my goodness, I've been having a hard time since my youngest went off to college. I'm not sure what a life coach is, but do you think you can help me?' He practically hired me on the spot. And he wasn't even my ideal client."

Why is this story so important for new coaches to hear? Because it shows you that even though you may choose and develop a particular "ideal client" as part of your marketing strategy, you do not necessarily exclude other clients, and it most certainly won't mean you won't attract others or that you shouldn't work with people who are simply an "okay" fit. In other words: You never have to turn anyone away! As long as you have room in your schedule, you can coach anyone you please.

Choosing a niche is about marketing.

It's about how you talk to people—about what you do as a coach—in a way that makes them listen.

In Donna's example, above, we honed her "pitch" so that she knew exactly how to answer the question, "What do you do?" in every type of circumstance. She no longer clammed up or stammered when talking about her work. She simply said,

"I'm an Empty Nest Life Coach," and it often piqued interest in a crowded room or even in a small group. The man at the party heard the words, "empty nest" and pounced, because he knew immediately that he wanted a solution to the problem he was having. He admitted he didn't even know there was help out there. You see? Had Donna simply said, "I help people who are in transition," she probably wouldn't have made a connection with this man. He wouldn't have paid attention.

You have to get inside the heads of your clients. What are they worrying about? They're certainly not saying things like, "I need a life coach," or, "I need a coach who will help me through my transition." No! They are saying very specific things, like, "I'm lonely. My house feels so empty." "I don't know what to do with myself. I don't know what to do without my kids around."

LIN M. ELEOFF

These are the sorts of things you would talk about on your Home page. And your About page. And your Work With Me page. Potential clients will think you're reading their minds and BOOM, you're hired.

Why? Not because you're a life coach but because you have a solution that will help them feel better. Everyone just wants to feel better. Tell them you're listening. Let them know how you can help.

Instead of, *"I'm a weight coach,"* say, *"I help women who are going through peri-menopause get a grip on their weight and even lose a few pounds while they're at it."*

The woman who is 47 and feeling like she's suddenly "losing her grip" and "gaining weight" is going to sit up and pay attention when she hears that message. But she probably won't pay as much attention if the message is, "I help women transitioning through menopause," because women who actually are transitioning through menopause don't say things like, "I'm transitioning through menopause." If you talk like that they're not going to listen.

Choosing a niche is about knowing how to talk so your market will listen.

As counterintuitive as it sounds, niching it down will set you apart from other coaches.

In my book, "Unleash That Niche," which I give to all my private coaching clients, I have a whole process that helps coaches figure out their target market and their ideal client within that market. Afterwards they have so much clarity it's easy for them to attract people they really want to work with.

They know what to write on their Home page. They know what to write on their About page. They know what to write about, period.

This isn't necessarily easy to do on your own, so if you're not nailing this, hire someone to help you, someone who knows how to pull it all out of you. It's *that* important. If you're not attracting enough clients, then you're obviously not making enough money, and that keeps you from experiencing the joy-*full* freedom you were hoping for when you became a coach.

ACTION STEPS:

1. Make a list of the things your ideal clients actually say when they talk about their problem.

2. Using their language, describe how you help people solve their problem:

   > For example: *"I work with gutsy, glorious life coaches who want to learn how to turn their life coaching practice into a soulful, money-making business—one that's fulfilling, meaningful, and a joy to wake up to every day."*

STEP 5: GIVE YOUR BUSINESS A (BLOG) VITAMIN

Ready, Set, Blog!

As in... start blogging. Right now.

If you think I'm kidding, look at my face.

It doesn't matter if you don't have a website yet. Please trust me on this one. You're going to thank me later. You may even want to send me chocolates! My private clients always hate this part, until they love it. And me. Never fails.

Write six blog posts in one week. Then six more the week after that. For a total of TWELVE blog posts in two weeks. *(Wait! Don't run off to The Land of WTF yet. Hear me out. Please?)*

I know. I know. I know. Blogging is hard.

No! Snap out of it.Saying that blogging is hard is like saying talking is hard.

When you have something to say, you speak. Blogging is just like that. You don't need to write prose. You don't have to be a grammar expert. In fact, even if you are an actual grammarian, please don't let it show. Write like you speak to ensure people will actually listen. This is no time for highfalutin pomposity. *(Is there ever a time for highfalutin pomposity?)*

If you're brand new to coaching, you've got to create some sort of presence on the Internet, and you've got to do it regularly. It's part of your "job," and if you're a good boss, you'll make yourself do it in a way that feels delicious for you. The bottom line: find a way.

LIN M. ELEOFF

Now, I realize we haven't even talked about building a website yet, so you may think I'm getting ahead of myself. I am not.

Write one blog post a day, *whether your website is ready or not.*

Think of it as a vitamin pill for your business.

The goal is to be ready to have *at least* 12 blog posts in the can, ready to go, when your website goes live.

Now, if you haven't nailed your niche, this could actually become a very painful process. Therefore, you must go back to Step 4 and do that work, if needed first. I promise you that you have a niche inside you. And if you really can't figure one out, then pick something that resonates with you, because over time, your niche will unfold. (I truly believe helping my clients "unleash that niche" is some of the most important work we do together.)

Then, here's what I want you to do. Pick a person you love talking to. It has to be someone you know who has a problem for which you have a solution.

What's her name? What's she like? Why do you like her? (Yes, you must like that person.) What does she struggle with?

How can you tell she's struggling? What does she say about The Struggle? What does she wish for? How will her life be different once the struggle is over? This is all fodder for your writing. (I realize it may not be a struggle, necessarily, that your clients are dealing with. Label it what you will.)

First, write 12 blog post titles that are relevant to The Struggle.

Next, write her a series of "letters" that tell her how much you can relate to The Struggle she's experiencing, and why.

Tell her about your own experience with this struggle and how you overcame it. Open up to her. What hope can you give her?

How many other people have this struggle? Assure her that's she's not alone. Explain to her how her struggle can actually be a profound gift that she'll come to appreciate once she does "the work" required to overcome it.

Now, turn all of the above into 12 ~~blog posts~~ letters. Start at the beginning, by describing what she's experiencing. Tell her how she's a lot like you, and like so many other women. Your letters do not have to be measured by the number of words; they can be short and concise, one flowing into the next. I think this is much more effective than one long diatribe of a post that is more likely to lose your reader's attention.

I assure you this won't be hard once you start.

But you must start.

And you must finish... *in two weeks.*

Don't overthink this.
Just write.

Your business needs its vitamins.

I use this fire-hose method with my private clients and they always protest at first. And then they're amazed at what they've accomplished. Yes, some posts are better than others, but that's not what matters. Success is measured by your ability to feel the fear and blog anyway. This may very well turn out to be the most fulfilling thing you ever do, no matter how messy and unpolished and raw it may be.

This isn't only about business. This is personal.

While I realize it takes guts to do what I'm asking, you already know you can do this. You *will* do this.

'Cause you're gutsy that way.

ACTION STEPS:

1. Open a new file folder and name it "Future Blog Posts."

2. Make a list of 12 blog post titles that tackle one particular aspect of "The Struggle."

3. Each day for the next two weeks, write at least one blog post to your Future Client—write it as if you were writing her a letter, or talking to her on the phone. (Note: you may find it easier to write 2 or 3 short posts a day, because you'll be in The Flow.)

STEP 6: NAME YOUR BUSINESS

Giving your business a name doesn't necessarily have to have anything to do with your brand. At the beginning stages, especially, I always suggest naming your core business after your actual name. This gives you greater bandwidth. For example, my business name is Lin M. Eleoff, LLC. I can use that name for any type of business I may choose, now or in the future.

If you're a Sole Proprietor, you have no choice but to use your actual name as your business name and then register a DBA ("doing business as") if you want to do business under a different name with a fully developed brand. It's so much easier to change a DBA than it is to change the name of an LLC or S-Corp.

So many coaches have started with fancy business names that they tire of after a year or so, and as they evolve and make other choices these names may feel limiting or even gimmicky. Your actual name, however, will be with you wherever you go. So keep it simple, use your name, at least to get you started. You can always register a DBA (also known as a "fictitious name" or "trade name") once you find a name for your business that you love.

In most states, registration of a DBA is done through the office of the Secretary of State or perhaps your county clerk's office, depending on where your business is located.

If you do choose a different name for your business, make sure it's a name that's easy to remember, easy to pronounce, and easy to spell. You don't want a name that's spelled differently than it sounds, especially if you're going to use it in a domain name (next chapter).

The only time you wouldn't want an eponymous company name is if you think you might want to sell your business later. The bottom line, however, is that there are so many different opinions about how to name your business, and I suggest not going down that rabbit hole at the beginning because it will keep you from getting other critically important stuff done. The point here is to get you started. You are likely going to want to make so many changes in the first two years of doing business online that it's best to just start. Right now.

One thing you want to be very careful of is not to choose a name that is already being used by someone else, or you could get slapped with an infringement suit. I've seen this happen far too many times. A fellow entrepreneur created a new product, bought a domain name for it, and spent USD $22,000 dollars getting it to market. Once he went live, he was promptly served with a cease and desist order. Turns out, there was another company using that name, and they weren't going to let him get away with infringing on their mark. That was a 22,000 dollar mistake that could've been avoided.

Make sure you research this, or better still, have a lawyer do a deep level search of all federal and state databases to ensure the mark you want is actually available for use. By law, the name you choose for your business cannot be the same as, or confusingly similar to, an existing corporate name or trademark. If there is a "likelihood of confusion," you'll be denied the right to use it.

ACTION STEPS:

1. Choose a name that is easy to spell (keep it simple).

2. Make sure it's not already taken, i.e., registered in your state.

3. Make sure it's not federally trademarked (See Step 31).

STEP 7: NAB A DOMAIN NAME THAT'S LEGALLY YOURS

Your domain name is your business's address on the Internet. Here's the most important thing you need to know about this: Make sure *you* are the person who registers the domain name, not your web designer or virtual assistant. This is so important. You want to ensure that you are the *registrant* and the "owner" of the domain name, even though "owner" is a misnomer since no one actually owns anything on the Internet.

If you do a "WHOIS" search (whois.icann.org) you'll be able to see the following information:

1. Registrant

2. Administrative

3. Technical

4. Billing contact

You want to see your information here, including your name, contact information (email), and mailing address. If you don't, you are not the actual registrant/owner[2] of that domain name. And that could become a problem. Several coaches I know, whose domain names were bought for them by their web designers/developers, lost their ability to use their domain names and the websites that were built for them because they got into a dispute with the people who had bought the domain names on their behalf. That's like having your real estate agent buy a property for you. Ultimately, the coaches in question had to wait until the domain names expired, all while hoping the web designers wouldn't renew the domain names out of spite. It happens!

I cannot tell you how many business owners have been shocked to learn their domain names don't belong to them. One sure-fire way to find out is to log into your web hosting company and try to access the "C-Panel." Consider it a big red flag if you can't.

---

[2] No one actually "owns" domain names because no one "owns" the Internet. It's more like a yearly rental that you are entitled to renew for as long as you want.

LIN M. ELEOFF

It's also important that you not share your log in information,
or if you do, make sure you can trust that person not to wreak
havoc with your site. It's tempting to think, "That'll never
happen to me," but that's usually when this stuff happens. Be
careful.

If you do run into trouble, ICANN may be able to help you.
As explained in "Know The Law" in Step 3, ICANN is the
organization that influences policy and laws governing the
Internet. It also oversees domain names and has created a
"Uniform Domain-Name Dispute-Resolution Policy." This
policy is designed to make it difficult for anyone to hold onto a
domain name that is completely unrelated to its core business.
If you need to reclaim ownership of your domain name,
contact ICANN. You might also consider consulting with an
attorney who specializes in Internet law.

ACTION STEPS:

1. Choose a domain name registrar that is ICANN
    accredited.

2. Register your domain name yourself using your email and
    other contact and payment information—don't let someone
    else do this for you.

3. Don't buy a .net if someone already owns and is using the .com.

STEP 8: GET SOCIAL + START A (GLORY) BAND

Once you know the gist of your new company's direction, you can start talking it up on the various social media playgrounds you like to participate in. You don't have to wait for a big launch. Start early and build momentum. Drop hints. Ask questions, perhaps even do an informal survey to find out if people have any ideas about your niche. If any of the participants turn out to fit the profile of your ideal client, consider them part of your Glory Band.

It's important to start such a band because, *who doesn't want to be in a band?* Your Glory Band will teach you so much about *how* your clients think and *what* they think about, exactly. This will ultimately help you serve your band in deep and meaningful ways. Maybe you can even write them a song, as one of my coach clients actually did.

One thing you really must do is set up a business page on Facebook. I know, a business page is not nearly as much fun as all the interaction you have on your personal profile page, but you'll *need* a business page if you plan to run any FB ads. And while it's much easier to get engaged with the people who are already your friends (or become friends) on your personal page, it is important to establish a presence for your business.

A word of caution: Be careful with how much you promote your business on your personal page. It's ok to talk about it, but overt selling is not allowed on profile pages and you could get shut down by Facebook. Your business page, on the other hand, is where you can go all out with promoting your stuff, but again, even though it's allowed, it's not good business practice to *only* use your business page for marketing purposes. Mix it up. Have fun. Make relevant conversation, include people. And don't be afraid to get personal on your business page.

If it helps, have themes for each day of the week: Mondays is for motivational quotes and articles; Tuesday might be about a topic related to your business or your blog post for the week; you get the idea. Having a system helps. But don't neglect your business at the expense of interacting on social media. I'm sure I don't have to tell you about that rabbit hole. Put a time limit on how much you'll spend online and stick to it.

One of the best Facebook business pages I know is Karen Salmonsohn's "Not Salmon." She is utterly delightful and I love sharing her motivational (highly creative) graphics on my page. Karen is the real deal and has found a perfect balance between personal and business. Check her out.

A last word of caution: Don't spread yourself too thin. I wasn't on social media until I started my online business, and I chose Facebook because that's where all my coach friends were—and it was easy for me to use. Twitter, for me, not so much. But, it may be the exact opposite for you. Pick one, however, and work it, as opposed to trying to be everywhere. Find one you like and stick with it until you've built some momentum. Participate in conversations. Add value wherever you can. And make sure you are consistent. Be consistent. Be consistent. Be consistent.

ACTION STEPS:

1. Choose one social media platform you enjoy participating on.

2. Create a page for your business.

3. Map out a simple and easy to follow system you can stick with.

4. Stick to the system each day.

STEP 9: GET AN EIN

In the same way that you, as an individual, have a Social Security Number (SSN) that identifies you as a taxpayer of the United States, so too must your business have a legal number.

A **Federal Tax Identification Number (TIN)**, or **Employer Identification Number (EIN)**, is a nine-digit number assigned by the IRS to business entities operating in the U.S. It identifies the person or persons who own the business, and how they can be contacted.

You can apply for an EIN online. It's free. And it's easy. Very easy, I promise. Just go to the IRS.gov website to register. You are eligible to apply for an EIN if:

1. Your principal business is located in the United States;

2. You have a valid Social Security Number or Tax ID Number.

Don't you just love it when the steps are this easy?

STEP 10: REGISTER YOUR BUSINESS NAME

If you've chosen a business name that is not your actual name, it's time to make it legally yours, unless someone else has beaten you to it. Remember, in most states, you are legally required to register your business unless you are a Sole Proprietor and are using your own name to do business.

Check with the requirements of your state's business/corporations division to make sure you're in compliance. The public policy interest behind having to register your business is to ensure that the general public is able to find out the identities of the players behind a company name.

Register your business with the appropriate government agencies in your state.

The easiest way to register a name if you're a Sole Prop is to file a DBA in your state, as discussed earlier in Step 7. LLCs and S-Corps are automatically registered upon creation.

Another reason to register your name is so that you can put your stake in the ground, preventing others from using that name, but this protection only applies after it is approved by

73

the state's business department. Keep in mind that you can only claim that name in the state in which it's registered; you won't have any protection in the other 49 states. To claim exclusive rights to the name across the country, you will have to register for a federal trademark.

ACTION STEPS

1. Check with your state business offices regarding registration requirements.

2. Register a DBA or your LLC or S-Corp (see next step).

STEP 11: BUSINESS ENTITIES 101

Your choice of business entity will impact your business in two major ways:

1. The amount you pay in taxes;

2. How well your personal assets are protected from liability.

A business entity is a legal structure established to create a separation between the "owners" of the business and the business itself. Most coaches start out as Sole Proprietors and then make the switch to forming a Limited Liability Company or a Sub-chapter S Corporation. We'll discuss each of these, and why they may be right for you down the road, but first I want to give you a little background info.

Corporations Overview

A tradition corporation (C-Corp) is an entirely separate entity from its "shareholders." Legally, a corporation is considered a "person" in the eyes of the law. This means that it's the corporation itself, and not its shareholders, that is held liable for the actions and debts incurred by the business. When it comes to taxes, C-Corps are dealt a double whammy: First, the corporation pays taxes on its annual earnings, and then any dividends incur income tax liabilities for the shareholders who receive those dividends, even though earnings tax was already paid at the corporate level.

The C-corp is for big companies with a lot of shareholders. It's not ideally suited for the small business owner.

LIN M. ELEOFF

The Corporate Veil

The corporate veil is a lot like a bridal veil–thin and
transparent–except you don't wear it on your head. (I'm sure
you knew that.) It's a legal concept that's intended to protect a
corporate shareholder from liability incurred by the
corporation. But if that veil is "pierced," the shareholder(s) can
be held personally liable for the company's debts and
wrongdoing.

So, keep this in mind as we discuss the differences between an
LLC and an S-Corp: Your choice of business entity will only
protect you as long as you stay on one side of the veil, and
keep your business on the other. For small business owners in
particular, that means keeping your personal assets (money,
bank accounts, expenses, investments, etc.) completely
separate from your business. As in, completely.

Now let's discuss the business structure that is best for you.

STEP 12: SOLE PROP VS. LLC VS. S-CORP

Sole Proprietorship

A Sole Proprietorship is not really a business "entity" because there is no differentiation between the business owner and the business itself. If you're doing business as a Sole Prop, you are the business, and the business is you.

A Sole Prop "springs into being" the moment of your first transaction (yes, it really is that simple). Sell your first coaching package or service and, voilà, you're in business. That's all it takes.

The problem with the Sole Prop (because you just knew it couldn't be *that* easy) is that it leaves you and your personal assets exposed to creditors who may have interest in your business. Because there is virtually no difference between *you* and *your business*, you pretty much have a target on your forehead—and your house, your bank account, your children's college fund, and all other personal assets you may own. That's because, as a Sole Prop, you're personally liable for any debts or wrongdoing related to the business. Of course, none of us plan wrongdoing, but mistakes and accusations can happen.

77

LIN M. ELEOFF

Ouch.

However, if you're just starting out, have limited funds, and have little risk of liability, then a Sole Prop may be all you need. Just make sure you **cover your assets with the right amount of insurance.** And when it comes time for you to break up with your Sole Prop (even though I know you love it, sadly, love isn't always enough), you can consider two legal entities: An LLC or an S-Corp.

The S-Corporation ("C-Corp Lite")

An S-Corp (it has a Sub-chapter 'S' designation in the tax code) is considered a "pass through" entity, because it does away with the double taxation whammy of the C-Corps. This means that all corporate income, losses, deductions, and credits pass through to the shareholder(s) for income tax purposes.

S-Corps can have no more than 100 shareholders and have only one class of stock, among other requirements (you must be a U.S. citizen and you can't be a bank or insurance company).

As the single shareholder or "owner" of an S-Corp, you must pay yourself a "reasonable" salary plus "distributions" from any additional profits the corporation may earn. Be careful here, because if you try to dupe the IRS by not taking what's considered a reasonable salary (so as to pay less in taxes), you risk piercing the corporate veil.

Similarly, if you commingle personal and business expenses, that lovely corporate veil could come tumbling to the ground and your company would then be treated as a traditional C-Corp and that means... double whammy at tax time.

The Limited Liability Company

The limited liability company (LLC) is a hybrid structure, offering many of the benefits of a Sole Prop with the limited liability protection that an S-Corp provides. This means you would file an individual tax return as the sole member/owner of the LLC. The LLC itself is not taxed. As a Single Member LLC, you'll be required to pay self-employment tax on any income derived from the LLC, which will require you to make quarterly estimated payments to the IRS.

Keep in mind that you risk losing your protection from liability if you pierce the corporate veil. Single member LLCs must take extreme measures to show the IRS that they're operating real companies, and are not just trying to dupe the system.

LIN M. ELEOFF

LLC or S Corp?

I knew you were going to ask me this. And while I wish it were otherwise, the honest answer is, "It depends."

The reason I'm hedging here is because each state has its own rules when it comes to regulating business entities. That's why I urge you to start by visiting the website of your state's Secretary of State to learn about the law that's relevant to you.

Generally speaking, however, an LLC has the advantages of being easy to form on your own. An S-Corp, however, is a more complicated structure, and it's best to seek the advice and services of an attorney familiar with the laws in your jurisdiction if you decide to go that route.

No matter what you decide, here's your BIG FAT TAKEAWAY: above all, don't mess with the IRS. Keep a meticulous set of books for your business, and do not commingle your personal and business banking. Instead of a veil, I suggest constructing a brick wall between you and your business. You know, so you can sleep at night.

A Word About Partnerships

A partnership is a way for individuals to combine their skills, knowledge and expertise to form a business that has a common purpose. When two or more individuals collaborate to form a business, a partnership is established. Partners may also contribute money, property, and time. There is an expectation that their efforts will generate profits, in which each will share. A partnership is formed with or without a formal agreement between the principals... all that's needed is the mutual will of the parties involved.

Partnership law is regulated by state statutes. Make sure you understand and comply with the laws of the state in which your partnership is formed.

There are two main types of partnership: the *general* partnership and the *limited* partnership.

Several federal and state requirements must be met in order to establish a legal partnership. **A legally binding written agreement, drawn up by an attorney, is strongly suggested, although not legally required.** Also, check the registration requirements of the Secretary of State where you live. Other regulatory requirements vary depending on the state and locality in which you live, as well as the industry in which you are doing business. Limited Partnerships limit the liability of the individual partners in much the same way an LLC limits the liability of its members.

ACTION STEPS

1. Visit the website of your state's business office or Secretary of State.

2. Make a list of the filing requirements, depending on your choice of business entity.

3. Set aside a block of time to fill out the paperwork.

4. File the documents online or by sending directly to the appropriate state offices.

STEP 13: OPEN SEPARATE BUSINESS BANK ACCOUNTS

Open a separate business banking account. Whether you're coaching full time or part-time, operating as a sole proprietor or an LLC, it's so important that you keep your business banking separate from your personal banking.

This not only gives you credibility as a business owner, it reduces your personal liability, and it most certainly helps you maintain control over your taxes, bills and how money is flowing in and out of your business.

The IRS has record-keeping requirements for income and tax deductions that require you to keep business and personal transactions separate in order to provide an easy audit trail.

Keep in mind that If your business is an LLC or S-corp, then maintaining a separate business banking account is vital: comingling your business and personal funds means that you're treating your business money as your own and that may be enough to "pierce the corporate veil"... which means there won't be anything to stop creditors from coming after your personal assets.

Besides, you can't deduct what you don't document. So keep your personal and business funds separate.

ACTION STEPS:

1. Choose a bank where you'd like to set up your business accounts.

2. Have your legal business name and EIN number with you.

3. Open a savings and a checking account in the name of your business.

STEP 14: SET UP A PAYMENT PROCESSING SYSTEM

If you're going to make money, you've got to have a system for taking payments. The easiest way to do this is by using a third-party merchant account (aggregators) like Paypal or Stripe, both of which service millions of people through one merchant account. Be aware that there are fees associated with using these services, and they can add up. At the time of this writing, the fees were all around the 3-percent mark (2.9% to be exact). There may also be additional transaction fees.

Using a third-party merchant account is good for anyone making less than USD $100 thousand a year. Once you cross that threshold you may want to consider getting your own merchant account (not shared with anyone else) in order to save a substantial amount in fees.

If you already have a personal Paypal account, open another one that's dedicated to business use only, and hook it up to your business bank account. You can then manually transfer funds from Paypal to your bank account. PayPal also has what's called an "Auto Sweep" feature for certain account types that allows you to transfer money from PayPal to a linked checking account automatically.

With Stripe, the transfers are done automatically by default, so as soon as you're paid, Stripe will make the transfer to your account; just be sure it's hooked up to a valid business checking account.

The problem with aggregators like Paypal and Stripe is that you still run the risk of them keeping your money or closing your account if you should have a sudden influx of funds. If you expect to have a spike in payments due to a product launch, for example, be sure to notify Paypal (or Stripe) in advance—not only to make them aware, but also to ask them about the likelihood of having your account frozen or shut down. Conceivably they could hold your funds for three to six months (or more) to make sure there won't be a sudden demand for refunds.

eChecks

An echeck (electronic check) is simply a digital version of the old-fashioned paper check—remember those? Payments by electronic checks allow for the direct transfer from one bank

---

account (your client's) to another (yours). This method is certainly cheaper because it saves you that hefty commission charged by payment processors like Paypal and Stripe. An eCheck fee is typically around .50 cents and there is no commission charged. Google "receive eCheck payments" and you'll find a number of services to choose from.

ACTION STEPS

1. Choose a payment processing system and set up a business account (don't use your existing personal Paypal account, for example).

2. Contact the bank at which you have your business account to set up an electronic checks payment system.

STEP 15: GET INSURANCE

It's a mistake to think that structuring your business as an LLC or an S-Corp automatically eliminates the need for insurance. Even if your business entity protects you from having your personal assets exposed, relying on the structure of your business to protect you from all liability is not smart. Liability insurance protects your actual business against losses, but you want to make certain that your personal assets are expressly protected against any losses your business may suffer.

Think of it as a safety net designed to protect you from unforeseeable risks that come with running your own business.

Errors and omission insurance, also known as malpractice or professional liability insurance, protects you from mistakes that cause harm to another individual. This type of insurance protects you from having to fund the entire cost of defending against a cause of action that results from alleged malpractice. Prices vary. A *lot.* You'll want to do your homework; talk to other coaches, and perhaps engage some insurance agents. If you don't know where to start, talk to your homeowner's and/or car insurance company and ask them who they recommend. Or ask Google. Start somewhere, but do start.

No ostrich impersonations please. This is the absolute worst time to put your head in the sand. If you're running a retreat or other type of off-site event, don't think you can rely on that venue's insurance policy. If you get sued, you won't be covered by another company's insurance, unless you get that agreement in writing.

Sadly, people get sued all the time, often for frivolous reasons. No matter how much you do business on the up-and-up, no matter how careful you are, nothing can stop someone from suing you if they are hell-bent on suing you. Even if it's just for spite, "trolling," or some other misguided reason. You don't have to have done anything wrong to be the target of a lawsuit. Whether it's for malpractice, or for copyright or trademark infringement, make sure you're covered against lawsuits that could cripple you, personally, financially, and emotionally.

ACTION STEPS

1. If you work from home, contact your homeowners insurance company, and ask them what your policy includes as far as conducting business in your home.

2. Ask your fellow coaches for names of companies that offer errors and omissions and/or premises liability insurance to life coaches.

3. Get insurance!

STEP 16: CREATE A BUSINESS EMAIL ADDRESS

You want to look profesh, right? Well then the last thing you want to do is use a Gmail or Yahoo or (heaven forbid) AOL account to send emails to your clients and customers.

It screams *"I don't take myself or my business seriously."*

What you need to do (upon pain of death) is set up an email using yourdomainname.com so that it looks like this: yourname@yourdomainname.com. See how much better that looks?

You'll also want to create something like support@yourdomainname.com or info@yourdomainname.com (or both) to use for your contact information on your website's contact page and legal docs. Before signing on with a web hosting service, check to make sure that one or more email addresses are included with your account—some charge extra. I highly suggest funneling your email addresses through Gmail. You'll do this by going into your Gmail account settings and adding a "pop3 account." Make sure you have the password you created when you set up the email address on your web hosting service. Once your info is verified, you will no longer have to sign into your website's email through your web hosting service.

Gmail takes over.

Muah!

ACTION STEPS:

1. Contact your web hosting service to see how many email addresses are included with your account.

2. Create at least two email addresses, one for your name and one to use for support purposes.

3. Consider funneling through Gmail.

STEP 17: START BUILDING A "BUSINESS KIT"

Do this, stat!

Get a binder (basic or beautiful, you decide). Label it: "[Business Name] Business Kit"

Put divider pages inside and label them as follows (or in any way that works best for you):

1. Business Formation/Registration Docs

2. Banking/Finances

3. Insurance

4. Websites

5. Certifications

6. Intellectual Property

7. Contracts

8. Website Info

9. Miscellaneous

Having a Business Kit will simplify things for you immensely when it comes to quickly finding information, such as your coaching certification (tab 5), your IRS EIN# (tab 1), a listing of your IP (tab 6), your business banking and Paypal account (tab 2), your state and local governments' website info (tab 4), etc. You'll likely have some of this info already stored electronically, but if you're like me, you like to have hard copies at your fingertips to look up in a flash. Besides, it beats having information scattered everywhere.

A Business Kit that's full of every important scrap of info you need will make keeping track of all aspects of your business much easier to do. No longer will you have those moments where it feels like you're running in circles trying to find where you put that one piece of paper you need *right now.*

STEP 18: CONDUCT A SURVEY

Think about this for a moment: how many products and services do you buy that seem to be made *just for you?*

I'd hazard a guess that's just about everything, or you wouldn't buy them. How is it that it was so perfectly made for you? Because the person who created it did some research, conducted a few surveys perhaps, to find out exactly what turns you on. What do you like? What don't you like? What problems are you dealing with?

When someone gets it exactly right, you don't even have to think about buying it—you're in. You've got your credit card out before they show you the 'Buy Now' button.

That's the beauty of surveys. They make sure you "get it right" when it comes to creating the products and services you're going to offer your clients. Because the last thing you want to do is guess what they want. No. No. You've got to *know* what they want.

And don't try to sell them what they need.

As coaches, we may know what our clients really need, but if you try to sell them that, you risk losing them. For example, don't try selling them "thought work" when what they're asking for is weight loss—you can talk about thought work in your program.

When you conduct a survey, you uncover all sorts of things you might never have imagined your prospects are thinking and worrying about.

Whether you offer a multiple choice survey, or ask deep and meaningful questions that elicit equally deep and meaningful responses, is entirely up to you, but survey you must.

The results you get will provide you with a snapshot of the things the people in your market want.

This information is like feeding kale to your business. Use this valuable feedback to inform your business decisions, such as, the design of your website and its content; what to create for your free offer; what to include in your workshop; what to put on your sales page.

Survey Creation Tips:

- Don't ask broad questions. Make it easy for people to answer a question by being specific; don't make them have to think too hard or they won't bother responding.

- Make sure not to ask (many) yes or no questions—they won't tell you very much.

- Create an incentive for taking the survey. SurveyMonkey allows you to automate that process.

- Advertise your survey everywhere:

  - On social media.
  - On your website, particularly at the end of your blog posts.
  - Inside your email marketing messages.
  - As part of your email signature.

Once your survey is done, be sure to thank respondents for their valuable feedback. Share with them the surprising things you may have learned. This promotes engagement, and lets people know how much you value their input.

Surveys are not difficult to set up: The simplest way is to send a few questions in an email or post on social media. You can also create a survey for free in Google Docs. You can even use a service like SurveyMonkey—some functionality is free and even more features are available when you pay for the survey or become a subscriber.

Finally, make sure your objective is clear when you create your survey. Tailor your questions so that you'll get responses on a specific topic, or from a specific demographic. Then have fun reading the responses. And be prepared to be surprised.

ACTION STEPS:

1. Determine your objective—what do you need to learn from the survey?

2. Create 3 to 6 questions that are specific to the topic.

3. Offer an incentive.

4. Put your survey out there.

5. Follow up with the people who took the survey, let them know what you learned, and thank them for participating.

STEP 19: CREATE A FREE OFFER THAT MAKES PEOPLE SALIVATE

Let me start by saying that the following words ought to be banned from your website: "Sign Up For My Free Newsletter." That may have worked a few years ago, but these days people aren't as willing to part with their email addresses—you've got to make it worth their while. How do you do that?

First of all—it's got to be relevant and consistent. Make sure you offer something that is related to the overall theme of your business because that's why someone is visiting your site in the first place. In other words, if someone comes to your site because they were expecting to find apples (because you were talking about apples on Facebook) but when they clicked a link they were brought to a page on your site that talked about oranges instead, they're going to hightail it out of there.

Next, keep it simple, quick, and tasty. Your free offer has to be bite-sized. Think of what happens when you're in a grocery store and they offer you free samples to taste—they don't give you a whole slice of pizza, they give you a small taste in the hopes that you won't be able to resist buying more. If that first bite is delicious, chances are you'll buy the whole pizza—all it takes is one delicious bite. That's what you need to do with your free offer; make it so tasty they'll want more. For example, a one-page checklist instead of 40-page PDF, or a five minute video instead of a 3-part video series. You want to make it easy for someone to "consume" your free offer quickly, and to provide them with an instant payoff.

Finally, you want your free offer to provide a solution to one small piece of the bigger problem your visitors are experiencing; you don't have to solve the whole problem, just a bite-sized piece of it. Let's say you're a lawyer who has products and services designed to help online business owners "get legal with it" when it came to protecting their business assets. A bite-sized offer might include a one-page checklist (*not* a 40-page PDF) called the *Ultimate Online Business + Legal Checklist,* something visitors to your website could download and immediately get a sense of what they had to do to protect their businesses. This quickly solves their immediate problem of *not knowing what to do or where to begin* when it came to starting an online business and protecting it.

Here are a few other examples of what you may offer:

- A quiz or questionnaire that helps them see something they were oblivious to before;

- A (very) quick instructional video that solves one piece of their problem puzzle;

- A 15 minute free consult; this is not a time for you to pitch your paid offer; this is a chance for you to deliver a sample of your coaching techniques, something that makes them say, "Wow, that was awesome! I never thought of it that way."

Of course, there are all sorts of things you can put in your free offer. Get creative. Show your personality. Have fun, but above all else, provide *value.* And remember, this is not a time to pitch your services. This is only the first dance. Give them a chance to get to know the dance steps without stepping on their toes.

ACTION STEPS:

1. Set aside time (half a day should do it) to create your free offer.

2. Keep it relevant, concise, and easy to consume—with an instant payoff.

3. Upload your free offer to your website's media library or include it in the email you send through your email marketing service provider.

STEP 20: CREATE A LANDING PAGE THAT CONVERTS

Whether or not you have a website, you can create a simple landing page for your free offer. In fact, I know businesses that don't even have a website—they rely strictly on a landing page to deliver a free offer to their website's visitors.

Think of a landing page as the front page of a newspaper.

It needs a **headline** that grabs the reader and pulls her in in about 10 words (or less). It's got to be irresistible, or you risk losing them.

You've got six seconds to make a promise you know you can keep.

That's it.

Six. Seconds.

Not to put pressure on your landing page or anything, but there's a lot riding on those first six seconds.

After the headline, you need a crushing **sub-headline**. Think of this as the delicious side of fries you love to have with that juicy burger. If the page's main headline is what grabs their attention at first, the sub-headline will be what makes their mouths water.

Put yourself in the position of someone who is looking for a coach. What is she looking for? What is her "problem"? How will you convey to her, in a headline and a sub-headline, that you know what she's thinking and feeling and that you can help?

It's a tall order, I know, but it's so important I suggest this is where you might consider hiring a copywriter to help you.

You can't afford to get this wrong.

Ideally, your landing page will also have an **enticing image** that conveys your message and your brand; something that will hook your ideal reader. In other words, it must be relevant. And it must *not* be a stock photo that screams, "This is a stock photo." You've got to use every inch of real estate on your landing page to show and tell your story in as few words as possible. If it's an image of you, please, please, *please* don't use one that your family took of you in the back yard or at a wedding, no matter how pretty you look, it will scream, "My family took this photo of me!"

I get it. There's a lot riding on your landing page. But how often have you visited a website only to click away in mere seconds? Conversely, how many times have you landed on a website and thought, "Whoa, this is cool. I want to know more?

A landing page only has one call to action. The reader is *never* confused about what she is being asked to do. There aren't multiple offers or different posts or articles to click on. The only thing people should be able to do on a landing page is sign up for something. *One thing.*

Bottom line: How can you make a statement with your copy and your image that says, *"I get you. I understand how you're feeling. I can help."*

And not to put more pressure on you but, it all has to happen "above the fold," which means you've got to get your message across without someone having to scroll down to find out what it means.

Your landing page is your big chance to connect. It's worth spending time and even some money on getting this right. It could pay big dividends in the future.

℘

Landing pages aren't just for your home page; they're for any page you want to send traffic to, or through. Traffic sources include ads, guest posts, social media shares, and email links, to name a few.

Having said all of the above, this, like so many other things in your business, does not fall into a one-size-fits-all category. As the market gets saturated with a certain "formula," you'll have to stay a step ahead. You see, your potential clients may be numb to the same old offers; the same old promises. It's your job to set yourself apart from the pack. Don't say the same thing as every other coach out there. Take chances. Get off the fence. Learn from your prospective clients; ask them what they're looking for and then *deliver it* in a one-two punch.

I offer you this strategy, like many of the guidelines in this book, as a jumping off point; a way to get you started. Don't be afraid to try new things. Test your ideas. If they work, great. If not, move on.

Trust your gut.

Serve your people.

ACTION STEPS:

1. Choose a simple landing page (available with most themes).

2. Write a headline.

3. Write a sub-headline.

4. Choose an image.

5. Connect the opt-in/sign up box to your email subscriber service (see next step).

STEP 21: CHOOSE AN EMAIL SUBSCRIBER SERVICE

You'll need to set up a service through which you can communicate (via email) to the people who decide to subscribe to your "list." Your list is comprised of all the people who have chosen to share their email addresses with you because they think your free opt-in is kickass. They have agreed to hear about your special offers and stay in touch.

Communicating with your list is *not* something you will do manually in Gmail or through your desktop because there are strict laws that put limitations on sending mass emails. In fact, Gmail itself will shut you down if you send bulk emails to people as a way of circumventing their right to subscribe and unsubscribe.

Marketing by email without consent is a no-no, and I'm not just talking about it being bad manners, it's actually illegal according to the FTC. That's why you'll need to enlist an email marketing/subscriber service such as MailChimp, AWeber, GetResponse, or ConvertKit, to name a few. Some services are free, but as with anything that is free, there may be limited features such as a subscriber cap and autoresponder capabilities.

Autoresponders, discussed two steps down, allow you to send an email sequence automatically. This feature becomes invaluable, as you will see, as your business grows.

ACTION STEPS:

1. Read up on the various email subscribers services.

2. Choose a service that meets your business needs.

3. Sign up!

STEP 22: BUILD THAT LIST

Want to avoid making one of THE BIGGEST MISTAKES most coaches (and online entrepreneurs in general) make? Then do exactly as I say here in Step #23 and thank me later (I like peanut butter cups, champagne, and lip gloss—always).

Once you have all the necessary pieces in place (and if you've done the previous 22 steps, you're ready) it's time to start building your email list.

Your business depends on it.

Why? Because having a large *and responsive* audience base is the key to your online success. And to create that large audience base, you've got to collect email addresses. The most effective way to collect those email addresses is to drive traffic to your Home Page, or a specific landing page you've created, and offer something so enticing, so utterly mouth-watering, that people will gladly hand over their email address to you in exchange.

You see, it's not enough to have a large following on Facebook or Pinterest or Twitter. When it comes to social media platforms, you're *not* in control, and if the platform should ever shut your account down, you're in big trouble—your followers will be gone, just like that. But an email list is a valuable asset that list belongs to you.

Generally speaking (and this will vary greatly depending on how "hot" your list is), about 3% of the people on your list can be expected to buy a product whenever you make an offer. That means (again, generally speaking) if you had 100 people on your list you could expect to make three sales. Do the math from there. How many people do you need to have on your list in order to generate the income level you desire?

&

So then, how do you "drive traffic," you ask? The easiest (fastest) way is to invest money in paid advertising, such as Facebook ads. Another way is to invest your *time* by working your butt off writing blog posts and creating content that will get you noticed by those Google Bots (see Step 24), which can and should include things like guest posting, guest podcasting, and simply being highly engaged on your favorite social media platforms. Make connections with other coaches or organizations whose niches complement yours.

There are too many list-building tactics to mention here but whatever you do, *build that list.* Spend time *every single day* devoted to driving traffic to a landing page where people can opt in to your list. And then, once they're on your list, treat them as if they were your best friends. Communicate with them regularly (at least weekly) by offering them great content that is relevant to their lives.

From now on, before you do anything, ask yourself, *"Will this help me grow my list?"*

ACTION STEPS:

1. Decide on a minimum number of people you want to add to your list on a daily, weekly or monthly basis.

2. Start experimenting with ways to drive traffic to your list.

3. Consider placing paid ads.

4. Adjust your strategy in order to hit your quota.

5. Once you hit your quota consistently, raise it.

STEP 23: CREATE AN AUTORESPONDER SERIES

An autoresponder series is a sequence of pre-written emails that are sent automatically to your email subscribers. For example, when someone opts in to receive your free offer, they are automatically sent an email (via your email subscriber service) that sets the sequence in motion. Now, you don't want to be selling *anything* at first: you want to establish a connection with that subscriber; you want to offer value; you want to start building trust, and you want them to get to know you.

None of this has to feel fake, phony, or inauthentic. It just has to feel like *you*.

You may use an autoresponder sequence to write a series of two to three emails that build on each other, and culminate in asking the subscriber to sign up for your free mini coaching session. You'll have to be the one to determine what feels best for you, but the more you can automate, the less pressure you'll feel to write emails on a regular basis, especially when someone is first added to your list.

For example, when someone signs up for my *Ultimate Online Business + Legal Checklist* on coveryourassetsonline.com, they receive the download automatically, followed by a series of high-value emails that will deliver more free content in the form of business and legal tips. Some online entrepreneurs even use autoresponders to deliver paid programs over a set period of days or weeks, in the case of group or self-study programs.

When you're just starting out, I suggest first setting up the following (short) autoresponder series that is triggered as soon as someone signs up for your free offer:

LIN M. ELEOFF

1. Free offer is delivered.

2. An automatic email is scheduled to be sent the next day, asking if they have any questions regarding the free offer. Invite them to reply to you, and assure them you will answer any and all questions. Add value by delivering an additional snippet of content in the email suggesting how they might further benefit from the free offer you sent them.

3. Another email is sent two or three days later inquiring again about their progress. Then, invite them to sign up for a free mini-coaching session with you (see Step 43), offering to help them figure out something that has them stuck. Assure them you can help them in only 15 minutes, and that the call is absolutely free and will absolutely *not* include a pitch for them to buy your product or service. (Hold this firm.)

You can keep adding to the sequence, or stop here. You can then have the subscriber automatically included to receive your regular weekly emails.

Whatever you do, make sure your content is beyond amazing and is full of value such that your subscribers cannot wait to open your emails. Pay attention to the "open rate" to gauge how well you're doing, and adjust accordingly. Also pay attention to whether you're able to engage your subscribers by inviting them to reply to your emails. This is often a very good indication whether you're hitting the mark, or not.

Finally, *do not ignore your list.* If you do, they'll be gone, and aren't likely to come back.

ACTION STEPS:

1. Write the first email people receive after signing up for your free opt-in.

2. Write a follow up email to be sent 2-3 days later, asking how they did with the opt-in.

3. Send valuable content 2-5 days after the last email; add a 'P.S.' inviting them to sign up for a free mini coaching session (to be discussed in Step 44).

4. Repeat step 3 as often as you'd like.

5. After 5-7 emails, consider doing a soft sell of a product.

STEP 24: GET "SEEN" BY THE GOOGLE BOTS

By now, you're well on your way to having at least 12 blog posts in the can and ready to go on launch day. Right? (I can tell whether you're nodding or not, Coach.)

I cannot stress enough how important this is to your business. Of course, it doesn't have to be in a blog—it can be a podcast (with a great intro and show notes so Google can find it) if you prefer, but you simply *must* have a way to communicate via your website on a regular (at least weekly) basis.

And I'm not just talking about communicating with your readers this time—I'm also talking about those adorable little "bots" that zip around the Internet reading content, taking notes, and then deciding where to put your blog in the search engine rankings. (Yep, they can read!)

Writing *text* is the only way to let those Google bots (and various other search engines) know you exist. You can't expect to be found by anyone if your website doesn't show up in the search engine results page (SERP), as in the page displayed by a search engine in response to a query by someone searching for a specific word, term, or phrase.

Before you can make an appearance on SERP a few things need to take place. First of all, your website must be "indexed" by a search engine. Indexing occurs when a search engine collects, parses, and stores data (from your text) for its own use. The amount of time this takes varies—depending on the site's popularity, whether the site is "crawl-able" by search engines, and how the site is structured. It's possible for a site to be crawled or indexed within a few days to several weeks, or not at all, depending on the variables mentioned above. Another factor in all of this is whether the site also contains what's called a sitemap.xml, which is a fancy shmancy bunch of code that tells the search engines how the pages on your website interlink with each other. Don't assume your content management system (ex., Wordpress) already contains a sitemap; check with your developer to make sure.

Here are some other things you can do to make sure your website is optimized so that those adorable Internet-crawling bots can find and read your site:

• Learn about Google Search Console (google it).

• Sign up for Google Webmaster Tools and follow the instructions, making sure to verify your site. This will help you monitor your site's performance according to Google.

- Consider hiring a webmaster to make sure you're doing it all right. This is complicated *and* time-consuming stuff. Also make sure said webmaster uses only "white hat" (legitimate) techniques to enhance your site's searchability. So-called "black hat" techniques will not only damage your site, but also your site's reputation and search rankings. This will take a very long time to recover from, measured in years.

- Get inbound links to your site. An inbound link is a hyperlink back to your site from another quality web site. Sites with high quality inbound links rank higher in the search engine results pages.

Now, remember, before any of the above can happen, you must have *content*. And the more content, the better, and the more often new content is added, even better still.

Which brings me back to the subject of blogging. You need to blog because you need to have text for the search bots to "read." Keep in mind that the bots can't read images and they can't listen to your podcast or watch your videos, so make sure you include regularly updated *text* in the form of *blog* posts and articles, or podcast and video show notes. Think of it like this: Every time you post, it's like inviting the bots to come for a visit. The more they visit, the higher you'll appear in the search engine rankings.

I realize I'm getting technical here but this is the kind of stuff you need to know so that you can figure out whether your virtual assistant or web developer knows about all this. Be sure to have discussions with whoever is responsible for setting up your website and make sure he or she is doing all they can to make it easy for the bots to find you.

Now, you may discover feelings of dread at the thought of putting your "voice" out there, which is more common than you may realize. But, once again, that's only a sign that another AFGO has come knocking—and that you need to haul your ass back into Thought Rehab. Because, in your heart, you know that you have something important to share with the world.

ACTION STEPS:

1. Write a blog post.

2. Write a blog post.

3. Write a blog post.

4. Repeat. On the daily.

STEP 25: SET UP YOUR HOME OFFICE

How awesome it is that you can just walk to your office without ever having to go outside, get in the car, maneuver traffic. And, the best part? Not having to take off your bunny slippers.

When it comes to your home office, there are rules and regulations you simply must be aware of. For starters, there are specific **zoning laws** that regulate how you can (or cannot) do business from your home. If you live in an area that's zoned as strictly residential, then there may be limitations on how you're allowed to run your business from home. There may be a limit, or an outright restriction, on having people work for you from your home, or from seeing clients in your home. Check with your local zoning authorities.

When it comes to qualifying for home office tax deductions, you must also meet the following IRS requirements.

1. **Regular and Exclusive Use:** These words are taken straight from the code and they mean that you must *regularly* use a designated part of your home *exclusively* for business purposes. If your bedroom doubles as an office because that's where your desk is, you likely won't satisfy the IRS's "regular and exclusive use" requirement.

There are two exceptions here: (1) If you run a daycare facility from your home, you are exempt from having to meet the "exclusive use" test. (2) If you store inventory or product samples in your home, you need not meet the "exclusive use" test.

2. Principal Place of Business: Your home office must be your principal place of business. That doesn't mean it must be your *only* place of business, but you must use your home office to do a substantial part of your business on a regular basis, even if you conduct meetings, for example, at a location outside the home. You may also deduct expenses for a free-standing structure on your home's property, such as a garage or studio or barn. In fact, the IRS likes this better, because it sets a much clearer boundary between "home" and "office."

Meeting Clients

Even if your home office doesn't meet the IRS criteria for doing business, you may still be able to claim deductions if you meet with clients in your home as part of the normal course of doing business. As long as the part of the home where you conduct such meetings is used exclusively and regularly for meetings with clients, you can deduct your expenses for that part of your home.

By the way, the use of your home for only occasional meetings and telephone calls will <u>not</u> qualify you to deduct expenses for the business use of your home.

To make this clear (I'm clarifying as fast as I can), the part of your home you use **exclusively and regularly** to meet clients or customers does not have to be your primary place of business; it's just that the part of your home where you conduct such meetings cannot be your living room or backyard patio; it has to be a place in your home that's *just for business use.* Anyone who steps foot in there for any reason other than your business is going to be in big fat trouble. (Kidding. Not kidding. Yes, I'm kidding.)

Likewise, you'll be able to deduct expenses for a separate free-standing structure such as a garage, studio, workshop, or barn, as long as (you know what's coming by now, right?) you use it **exclusively and regularly** for your business. Again, the structure doesn't have to be your primary place of doing business or a place where you meet clients, you just can't use it for non-business related activities as well, or *goodbye home office deduction.*

Home Office Deduction Methods

The IRS gives you a couple of options when it comes to calculating your home office deduction. Ask your accountant which method yields the best outcome for you.

Method 1: IRS "Safe Harbor" Method

If you use this method, 300 square feet will get you $1500 dollars in tax deductions.(Sounds like a popular car insurance commercial, doesn't it?)

In 2013, the Internal Revenue Service (IRS) announced a more simplified (safe harbor) option for deducting the business use of the home, commonly referred to as "the home office deduction." The optional deduction is based on a $5 per square foot deduction for up to 300 square feet, for a maximum deduction of $1500.[3]

Note: If you are an employee who uses your home to conduct business on behalf of your employer, and if you are reimbursed by your employer for such use, this deduction is *not* available to you.

---

[3] As of the time of this writing.

Method 2: IRS Standard (Form 8829) "Actual Expenses" Method

The old standard method of determining what you will be allowed to deduct has more calculation, allocation, and substantiation requirements that many small business owners find more burdensome.

First, calculate the total square footage of your home. Next, calculate the square footage of the space used for your home office. Then, calculate the percentage of the home that's dedicated to office space. Like this:

Square footage of office ÷ total square footage of home x 100

= _____ %

Example: 335 sf ÷ 2483 sf x 100 = 13.5 %

A bonus to using the standard method is that you will be able to fully deduct your direct expenses, unlike the Safe Harbor Method, for which there is a cap on deductions. You are strongly advised to consult with a tax professional when filing your annual return, especially when it comes to the types of deductions you're allowed to include.

ACTION STEPS:

1. Dedicate space in your home office to be used regularly and exclusively for business.

2. Check local zoning laws, especially if you will be seeing clients in your home.

3. Get insurance.

4. Choose a method of deduction for income tax purposes.

STEP 26: DON'T MESS WITH THE IRS

Since you don't have an employer taking taxes out of your paycheck, you'll have to pay the IRS yourself. Pay close attention here.

Self Employment Tax

Self-employed individuals are required to pay self-employment tax as well as income tax. SE tax is a Social Security and Medicare tax for individuals who work for themselves. Don't skip this or you may not be entitled to future benefits—and also because *it's the law.*

Income Tax

How much you'll need to set aside to pay income tax will depend on your tax bracket. There are several tools online to help you determine your tax bracket; simply google, "determine my tax bracket." This is the amount you will want to set aside for the IRS.

Another option is to commit to putting aside 30% of your earnings in a business savings account, and then pay the actual amount due at tax time.

Depending on your income level, it may be a good idea for you to pay estimated taxes. That's because federal and state governments prefer to not have to wait to get their (your) money and would rather receive installment payments on a quarterly basis. If you hold back on paying large sums, you could incur penalties and fees associated with "underpayment of estimated taxes."

Safe Harbor Rule

As long as you pay at least 90% of your estimated tax bill for the year, you'll remain in the IRS's good graces. There's also the Safe Harbor Rule which ensures you won't be charged any penalties or interest as long as you pay the IRS *this year* what you paid *last year* in taxes. In other words, your estimated taxes will be either: 90% of your estimated earnings in the current year, or at least the same amount that you ended up paying in taxes last year.

Most people choose to use 100% of the tax bill for the preceding year as the "safe harbor" amount; it's just easier to calculate, and is not likely to throw up a red flag.

If you're making considerably more this year over last year, consider paying more on a quarterly basis to show you're making a good faith effort to pay your taxes.

Take note: if your income exceeds $150,000 per year, then the rule changes a bit: the IRS expects you to pay 110% of last year's taxes to avoid penalties.

Remember, too, that you claim deductions for **startup costs** (things you had to pay for *before* you started making money) once you *actually start making money*, even if those costs were incurred before you got paid. Regular business expenses are those that were incurred *after* you started getting paid. So hold onto your receipts (even if from the previous tax year), because you will eventually get to deduct those expenses. Be sure to speak to your accountant or tax advisor about this.

LIN M. ELEOFF

ACTION STEPS:

1. Calculate your estimated earnings.

2. Determine what your tax bill will be, to your best estimate, or...

3. Set aside at least 30 per cent each time you get paid and put it in a separate tax savings account.

4. Pay self employment tax.

5. Calculate deductions.

6. Make sure you have a proper bookkeeping system (see next step).

STEP 27: COMMIT TO A BOOKKEEPING SYSTEM

The IRS requires that you keep records (including receipts) in order to claim your business expenses—make sure they're impeccable.

An impeccable set of books will:

- Help you keep track of your business's past and present performances and allow you to get a clear picture of how you're growing.

- Make it easy for you to find a receipt or invoice should the need arise.

- Make it supercalifragilistically easy for you to prepare your taxes each year!

I cannot stress enough how critically important it is for you to keep an organized and accurate set of books, i.e., one that includes a complete record of all the money that flows into and out of your business.

And yet... for some of us, it's the most loathsome part about running a business. At least that's what your petulant Child Mind will keep trying to tell you. To wit...

I don't wanna.

I hate this stuff.

It's too complicated.

I'll do it later.

This is so boring.

I hate math!

This is a time when you absolutely want to put your dear sweet inner 6-year-old in a corner until it's time for her to take *you* out to play. Under no circumstances are you to respond to her pleas to, *"Put me in, Coach."*

Manual vs. Electronic Methods

Manual bookkeeping systems include hard copies of all transactions with a set of books in which everything is entered by hand. Manual systems may seem to take more time but they are often ideal for anyone who isn't comfortable using computer-based programs.

If you prefer to get tech-y with it, there are several online applications that will keep track of your expenses, link to your credit cards, categorize purchases, ~~and cook you dinner~~.

You'll eventually want to consider hiring a bookkeeper, especially once your business starts to grow, or if you just can't make yourself follow through consistently, or if all of the above starts giving you a rash. Make sure you hire someone who specializes in tax filing and stays up to speed on the ever-changing tax code. Also, be sure to get a few referrals and conduct interviews to make sure the relationship is a good fit. If you can meet in person, all the better.

Also, consider hiring an accountant for tax time, since the tax code changes every year. Hiring an experienced accountant ensures you stay in compliance with current tax laws, including the ones in your state.

Bottom line: Do not wait until tax season to start your bookkeeping system. That's a surefire way to make you want to fire yourself for being a lousy boss.

ACTION STEPS:

1. Immediately start keeping track of the money that comes in and the money that goes out.

2. Choose (and stick to) a bookkeeping method that works for you.

3. Have a place to collect receipts (itemize and categorize).

4. Review your books monthly, at least.

5. Consider hiring a bookkeeper.

STEP 28: INTELLECTUAL PROPERTY 101

Let's talk "IP" shall we? You know, like the cool kids.
Intellectual property is lawyer-speak for "creations of the
mind." That means any original thought or idea that comes out
of your head—such as a blog post, a drawing, a photo, a work
of art, website copy, a book, an invention, a business name, a
tag line, a design, a program, a course or workshop, an audio
or video recording—belongs exclusively to you.

In short, IP encompasses all the assets you create for your
business, even if those assets are in digital form. If you wrote it,
took a picture of it, drew it, painted a splat of it with spaghetti
sauce on canvas, made a graphic of it or drew stick figures for
that matter, if "it" is your creation, you have the legal right to
protect it.

One thing to note: A mere idea (a thought) cannot be legally
protected because there's no way to copyright, trademark, or
patent your brain—or what's in it for that matter—so if you
don't yet have it "created", you'd best keep your idea a secret
until you can properly protect it with a copyright, trademark, or
patent.

And if you're even *thinking* about putting your idea into words, i.e., telling someone about your "secret," make sure to get a signed NDA (**non-disclosure agreement**) beforehand. Similarly, if you do hire a sub-contractor to make or create something for your business, be sure to also get it in writing that anything they create on your behalf belongs entirely and exclusively to you, and not the sub. This is so important I cannot emphasize it enough, so I'm going to say it again with some extra emphasis: *If you hire a sub-contractor to put your idea in a tangible form, make sure you also <u>get it in writing</u> (and signed by the sub) that anything they create on your behalf belongs entirely and exclusively to you.* This is called a **works-for-hire clause.**

In a nutshell, until you are able to legally secure your original work, you and your IP are vulnerable and you should take great lengths to protect.

The United States recognizes four different routes for protecting intellectual property: **copyright, trademark, patent, and trade secrets.** It is possible to obtain multiple forms of protection for the same IP. Considering that IP has the same attributes as real and personal property, it can be purchased, assigned, licensed or transferred.

LIN M. ELEOFF

Differences in IP Protection

The difference between copyright, trademark, patent and trade secrets lies solely in the type of *content* that each protects.

Broadly speaking, **copyright** protects original works of authorship (a book, for example), while **trademarks** are words, names, symbols, slogans, and designs that serve to distinguish the brand of one company from that of another. Patents protect inventions.

U.S. **patent** law states that any person who *"invents or discovers any new and useful process, machine, manufacture, or composition of matter, or any new and useful improvement thereof, may obtain a patent."* The key word is "useful." Anything deemed to be useless to the public is not considered patentable.

Trade secrets protect confidential (secret) information that gives one company an advantage over its competitors. Trade secret protection only protects *the secrecy* of such things as a formula, pattern, or device, but only against those who have agreed, expressly or implicitly, not to disclose the secret information, or against those who obtained the secret information illegally.

For purposes of this book, we will dive further into copyright and trademark protection as these forms of IP will likely be the best options for you when it comes to covering your assets online.

ACTION STEPS:

1. Make a list of all your business "assets."

2. Determine what, if anything, you'd like to formally protect.

3. Use non-disclosure agreements if you discuss new ideas with anyone.

4. Have sub-contractors sign a work-for-hire agreement.

STEP 29: COPYRIGHT

A copyright protects original, fixed, and tangible expressions of an original artistic idea, including books, articles, blog content, movies, songs, paintings, sculptures, images, photographs, dance choreography, computer software, and architectural drawings, sculptures, and dance. A copyright gives its owner (a.k.a. the creator of the original work) the right to choose whether her creations may be reproduced and how they may be shared, displayed, distributed, or performed. As well, a copyright owner has the right to allow or disallow derivative works (creations based on the original works of authorship).

Under common law, a copyright is automatically created once it becomes fixed in a tangible form. Let me repeat that: **As soon as you create an original work of authorship, a copyright is created.** You alone have the right to use that creation in any way you see fit, and that includes restricting others from reproducing, copying, sharing, posting, and otherwise using your work in any manner whatsoever, including "sharing" it on their website. And merely giving you attribution is not enough to thwart an infringement cause of action. Without express permission from you, no one can use your material without your consent, no matter how much they attribute the work to you, and vice versa: You cannot use someone else's work simply because you gave them attribution. Without express permission or a license, no one can legally use the original work of another.

Copyright Notice

You are strongly advised to place a copyright notice on all your original works of authorship, starting with the "small c with a circle" symbol (©). It also matters that you follow copyright notice convention, which looks like this:

© 2016 Lin M. Eleoff, LLC

Notice that the copyright symbol is followed by the year of the first publication of the work, followed by the owner of the copyright. A copyright notice prevents someone from claiming "innocent infringement" as a defense against a charge of stealing your work. But here's where the waters get muddied: you cannot sue someone for copyright infringement unless you have a *federally registered* copyright. And you can't simply backtrack and file for federal registration after the fact.

The bottom line, it's really difficult to sue for copyright infringement without federal registration of the copyright. However, if registration is made within 3 months of publication of the work, or prior to an infringement of the work, statutory damages *and attorney's fees* will be available to the copyright owner in court actions. Lastly, if you don't register your copyright *within five years of publication*, the court may not recognize your registration as evidence of the validity of the copyright.

LIN M. ELEOFF

Fair Use

Fair use is a legal doctrine whose purpose is to promote freedom of expression by allowing for the use of copyright-protected works *in certain circumstances,* without permission from the copyright owner. The Copyright Act identifies examples of certain types of uses that would be deemed fair, for example: criticism, commentary, news reporting, teaching, scholarship, and research.

Be careful, however, because courts evaluate fair use claims based on the particular facts of each case. This means you cannot rely on the number of words or lines of copy to determine what is deemed to be "fair." There is no formula to follow in order to ensure your use of someone else's work is fair. And as I said earlier, it's not enough to simply give attribution because it is always up to the original author or creator of the work to determine whether his or her work can be used by another.

A Note About Copyrighting Your Website

Merely putting a copyright symbol at the bottom of your website does not give you full copyright protection of your site's content. Full protection requires timely federal copyright registration, and when it comes to websites in particular, there are a few things to consider:

- First of all, you cannot copyright your website's domain name–that would require trademark protection.

- Secondly, copyright protection is only available for "original works of authorship." You cannot copyright someone else's work of authorship on their behalf, even if it appears on your website.

- Finally, copyright protection can only cover the parts of your website that you submit or "deposit" with the federal copyright office along with your registration.

Regarding that last one, any content you add to your website *after* registering your copyright will not be protected by the federal registration. You will have to file for copyright registration of the new content. In some cases, a frequently updated online work may qualify as an "automated database." A group of updates, published or unpublished, to a database (your website), covering up to a three-month period within the same calendar year, may be combined in a single registration. All updates from a three-month period may be eligible for registration with a single application and filing fee.

Registering a copyright is definitely something you can do without having to hire a lawyer. The fastest and most cost-effective way for a basic registration is to register online through the electronic Copyright Office (eCO). Go to copyright.gov and select "register copyright."

ACTION STEPS:

1. Post copyright notices on your website, as well as on your programs and services.

2. Federally register a copyright within three months of its creation in order to be able to sue someone for copyright infringement.

   • Complete an online application form.

   • Pay the nonrefundable filing fee.

   • "Deposit" your work (Yes, it's called a deposit, like depositing money in the bank). This is nonreturnable.

STEP 30: WHEN TO USE THE (DREADED) DMCA TAKEDOWN

If you feel someone has infringed your copyright or trademark, the first step is to send them a cease and desist letter. If that doesn't work, it's time to bring out the big guns.

The Digital Millennium Copyright Act (DMCA) provides a means for website owners whose content has been copied and used on another website without permission, to order the content be taken down by the Internet Service Provider (ISP) that hosts the infringing website.

ISPs dread receiving a DMCA Takedown Notice but are usually willing to adhere to the order to take down the infringing material because they could be held liable for allowing the illegally published content to remain on the infringer's website.

A DMCA takedown notice is the next step that a website/copyright owner would take after a cease and desist letter was sent directly to the infringing party (website owner) who failed to comply with the order to remove the content.

ACTION STEPS:

These are the elements of a properly formatted DMCA Takedown Notice:

1. Make the subject matter clear: "Notice of DMCA Copyright Infringement," for example.

2. Identify the copyrighted material and yourself as the copyright holder.

3. Identify where the infringing material is located (website and exact URLs).

4. Include proof that the content is your original work.

5. Include a Good Faith and Perjury statement that the information contained in the notice is accurate and true, and that you are signing the document "under penalty of perjury."

6. Sign the document (an e-signature is allowed) and provide your contact information.

STEP 31: TRADEMARK

Like I always say, *"If you like it, then you'd better put a trademark on it."*

A trademark is a word, phrase, tag line, symbol, logo, or design that identifies and distinguishes a company, a product, or a service, from that of another. Essentially, trademarks protect a company's brand identity—its identifiable marks—and prevents them from being used by others in the marketplace. A trademark lets the consumer know the *source* of goods. For example, when you see a swoosh symbol on a pair of shoes, you know those shoes are from a company named *Nike* and not from *Adidas.*

Like copyright registration, a federally registered trademark allows the owner to sue others for trademark infringement in federal court, and gives the owner of the mark the power to prevent others from distributing goods that display the trademark or "pretend" to be a product of the company that owns the mark.

Establishing Your Trademark

A trademark can be established in one of two ways: 1) federal registration or, 2) *actual use in commerce* (common law).

"Actual use in commerce" means that, similar to copyright, the moment you start using the trademark, you own it, *as long as no one else beat you to it.* If you're absolutely certain you're the *first and only* one using the mark, put a trademark symbol (™) on it. This lets others know that you have staked a claim to the mark *but it does not mean that the mark is federally registered.*

A federally registered mark will display the trademark registration symbol, the letter 'R' within a circle (®). You are not legally allowed to use this symbol until you receive an official trademark certificate from the USPTO.

Most federal registrations are now filed electronically through the Trademark Electronic Application System (TEAS) at uspto.gov/trademark.

Common Law Trademark Rights

Without federal registration of a mark, you have *common law rights*, which are limited to the geographic area in which the mark is used. For example, if you have staked a claim to "Equinox Equity Equus Coaching" in Portland, Maine, *there's nothing stopping someone else* from staking a claim to the same name for their coaching business in Portland, *Oregon*. However, neither coach could open a competing business in the other's territory, using that name. The rest of the country, however, is up for grabs. Bottom line, federally register your mark for maximum protection.

Search For "Likelihood of Confusion"

The standard for establishing your right to use a mark is that there must be no "likelihood of confusion"— the likelihood that your mark will be mistaken for that of another. Do a preliminary "knock out" search to determine whether the mark is already in use by another company by conducting a search on as many search engines as you can—Google, Bing, Yahoo, Ask, etc., as well as on big sites like Amazon and iTunes.

Next, do what's called a "TESS" search (Trademark Electronic Search System) at tmsearch.uspto.gov. It's a free search tool of the USPTO online database where you'll find text and images of existing marks as well as any marks in pending and abandoned applications. Next you'll need to check the Secretary of State corporations' database of the state in which you're registered to do business, as well as any other state in which you're conducting business. Finally, before you go buying up a bunch of domain names, always do a thorough search on whois.icann.org to make sure the name isn't already taken or in use.

Once you're satisfied that no one else has beaten you to it, it's time to consider federal registration. It's a good idea to consult with an attorney as the trademark application can be a complex and lengthy process. Also, if your application is incomplete or filed improperly, you'll face delays and possibly outright refusal of your application. An attorney will also be able to conduct a deep level search to rule out any possible conflict.

Whether you do it yourself or hire an attorney, plan for a year, at a bare minimum, to complete the process, sometimes shorter, often longer. While I've seen some applications go through in a matter of months, it's not typical.

ACTION STEPS:

1. Conduct a web search using Google, Yahoo, and other search engines.

2. Do a USPTO "TESS" search by going to tmsearch.uspto.gov.

3. Search the corporations database of the Secretary of State wherever you conduct business.

4. Do a thorough domain name search on whois.icann.org.

STEP 32: SAY "CHEESE" BUT DON'T BE CHEESY

There is no delicate way to say this, so I'm just going to say it, IN ALL CAPS...

DO NOT USE CHEESY PHOTOGRAPHS OF
YOURSELF ON YOUR WEBSITE. ESPECIALLY THE
ONES THAT WERE TAKEN BY YOUR KIDS, YOUR
FRIENDS, YOUR MOM, ESPECIALLY IF IT'S
OBVIOUS THAT YOU'RE SITTING AT YOUR
KITCHEN TABLE, OR THAT YOU'RE IN YOUR
BACKYARD (BECAUSE THERE IS A TREE AND
PATIO FURNITURE IN THE BACKGROUND). EVEN
IF YOU THINK YOU LOOK REALLY PRETTY IN THE
PICTURE, IT WILL STILL SCREAM "AMATEUR"
BECAUSE IT WAS NOT TAKEN BY A
PROFESSIONAL, I.E., SOMEONE WHO KNOWS
ABOUT DESIGN AND COLOR AND LAYOUT AND
LIGHTING. ALSO, DON'T USE PHOTOS FROM TEN
YEARS AGO OR FROM A TIME WHEN YOU WERE
TEN POUNDS THINNER OR ANY PHOTO THAT IS
MORE THAN ONE YEAR OLD FOR THAT MATTER.

Forgive me.

That was a bit of a rant, I'll admit.

Please, please *please* treat yourself to some pro photos. It
makes such a difference to the quality and professionalism of
your site (not to mention that it's fun to do). Plan to wear a
couple of different outfits so that you can mix it up on your

LIN M. ELEOFF

Home, About, and Work With Me pages as well as any PR
information you distribute.

I'm not talking glamorous.

I'm not talking photo-shopped to the hilt.

I'm simply saying, "be pro" and put your best face forward,
along with your personality and dazzling smile.

And here's a tip if you're wondering who to hire that won't cost
you more than you can spend: Call some of the wedding
photographers in your area. Their peak business days are the
weekends, so you can probably negotiate a good deal in their
"off time."

Or call around to your local colleges and see if there are any
photography students that would like to make a little money
while "practicing" on you.

Get creative.

Get pro photos.

Get pro photos.

Get pro photos.

ACTION STEPS:

1. Search for possible (wedding) photographers in your area.

2. Make an appointment. (Right now!)

3. Wear 3-4 different outfits, choosing colors that will complement your website (or go with black and white).

4. Choose at least 5 or 6 shots to use on your website and in your marketing materials.

5. No backyard family shots, please!

STEP 33: THE ABSOLUTE BARE-BONES BASIC BUSINESS PLAN

What I'm about to show you is what I call the *Absolute Bare-Bones Basic Business Plan.* Quite simply it's this: Know. Your. Numbers.

That's the plan. And it works. Perhaps you were expecting a 50-page doc? *No. No. No.* It doesn't have to be so complicated.

LIN M. ELEOFF

Having a complete understanding of the numbers that drive your profits is critical to growing an online business that you not only love, but that also *makes you money.*

All too often, coaches get caught up in *everything but* the numbers—blogging, web design, social media, newsletters—without having any idea what they actually have to *do* on a daily, weekly, and monthly basis, to generate the income they need and/or desire.

Online business owners who know their numbers are the ones who are the most successful, hands down. Why? Because this insight forces them to have a plan.

Do you know exactly how much money you want to make this year? Do you know exactly how you're going to hit that target?

When you know these numbers, you can then...

- Know how many clients you'll need to sign up.

- How many units of your product you'll need to sell.

- How many hours you'll need to coach each week.

It's not hard to figure out what your numbers are. But it does require some guts to commit to hitting those numbers. Let's get started. Pull out your calculator and a sheet of paper.

1. How much do you want to make over the next twelve months?

2. List the products and services you offer and the prices.

3. How many units of each product or service can you sell in one month?

4. Multiply the dollar amount in #2 by the number of units in #3.

5. Compare the total in #4 to the total in #1; What is the difference?

6. Do this for each of the products and services you plan to offer.

Once you determine your earnings goal for the year, fill in the blanks of the equation below for each of the products and services you offer.

$_____ (Price of product #1) x _____ (# of Sales Per Month) x 12 months = $_____ Annual Sales

LIN M. ELEOFF

This exercise shows you, in black and white, what you need to do to achieve your income goals for the next twelve months. Be realistic: consider how many products and services you *already have* to offer for sale; what other products or services you could *create* to increase your monthly income target; be sure to budget *how much time* it will take to create those offers. Taking all of those things into consideration, do you need to adjust your 12-month sales target?

When I did this exercise with a coach client named Shannon, she was shocked. She said she wanted to make $60,000 in the next **12 months**, but had no idea what that would entail. She didn't think it would be all that difficult. She had an existing one-on-one 6-week coaching package that cost **$497**. Even though she was just starting out, she believed that, "conservatively speaking," she could sell **5** packages every month:

$497 x 5 = $2485 per month x 12 = **$29,820**/year

When Shannon realized that would only get her halfway to her goal, she felt deflated. She also knew it would take her a while to double her sales. She chose to have a mini meltdown wherein her Child Mind threw a fit:

I didn't think that making $60k would be that hard. What the fuuuuuuuuuuuuu...

148

How am I ever supposed to do this?

I hate maaaaaaaaaaaaaaaath!!!!!!!!!!!

I have to admit, that's one of the tamer tantrums I've witnessed. (Mine included.)

Luckily for Shannon, she was able to use the *Extreme* Self Coaching process to quickly get back into Adult Mind. Subsequently, we came up with a plan for Shannon to create a passive income product that would not take up more of her time on a weekly basis (except the time required for her to create). If she priced that product at $147 and could sell 10 units a month, how much closer could she get to her $60k number?

$147 x 10 = $1470 per month x 12 = **$17,640**/year

This would bring her income up to $47,460 over 12 months; still short by $12,540, or about $1000 per month. Shannon decided that rather than try to *do* more (create more products, up her advertising budget), or *sell* more, she would adjust her 12-month income projection down to what she considered to be a more realistic goal of $50,000. Had Shannon not done this exercise, she would've felt lost for the next 12 months— another disappointed coach without a plan to develop her business.

Whether you're a brand spankin' new coach, or you've been flying by the seat of your glorious pants for awhile, you simply *must* know your numbers, all the time. This is your absolute bare-bones basic business plan.

ACTION STEPS:

1. Determine how much money you want to make in the next 12 months.

2. Make a list of your products and services.

3. Run each of them through the formula.

4. Make adjustments as needed.

STEP 34: LAUNCH, GROW, AND PROTECT YOUR WEBSITE

Before you can build a website, you'll need to know where you're going to put it.

You need to choose a **platform**. Because, after all, your website needs to run on *something*. Luckily, no one has to build a website from scratch anymore. You *will* need to make sure that you can easily manage your site, including doing simple things like uploading a blog post.

Enter, Wordpress. There are other platforms out there, but Wordpress is, by far, the simplest and once you get your website up and running, it's all yours—you have complete control. Find a theme you love, find someone to load it up onto a hosting service, and you're off to the races. The less customization the more you'll be able to go in and do things without having to *pay* someone *every* time you want to make a change on your site. That will add up to a lot of money *and hassle.* If you can fill out web forms, you can manage a Wordpress content system yourself, I promise. My web developer makes low-cost and beautiful websites for my clients and gives them instructions on how to post their blogs, upload photos, etc.

Next, you'll need to choose a **web host.** Think of a web host as the "land" you will rent to do business (with your website being the equivalent of a bricks and mortar storefront.)

Before signing up for a particular web hosting service, make sure you know the differences among the kinds of services available to you. This will all depend on things like your budget, your design needs, support services offered by the web host, and personal preference. Your web developer/designer can help you with this. These are your main options:

Free Hosting

Free web hosting is best suited for personal websites with low traffic expectations; it's generally not recommended for business sites. Sometimes these sites are supported by banner advertising that visitors to your site will be exposed to. Often in these cases, you'll be assigned a sub-domain that's not necessarily easy to remember or very professional, for example: yourname.freewebhost.com. Your ability to customize a free hosted site is often limited to the templates the host company offers. Something else to keep in mind, you'll likely not be able to simply transfer these free subdomains to another hosting site, paid or otherwise, in the future. It gets tangled up and a little messy. Plus, support is minimal.

Shared Hosting

Shared hosting is the most cost-effective hosting service because you're sharing the same server with other website owners, as well as the software applications that exist within the server. Shared hosting is good for you if you own your own domain name and have low to average traffic visiting your site. One of the major downsides is exposure in terms of security because of so many sites on the same server. If one of the other sites is targeted, your site could be affected. Some shared hosting services offer server upgrades for an additional cost. Popular shared hosting services include Godaddy and Bluehost.

Dedicated Hosting

Dedicated hosting is usually reserved for big businesses that can afford the cost of operating and acquiring a dedicated server. With a dedicated host you have the advantage of faster speeds and higher security. Because you have the entire web server to yourself, your site will run faster, you'll have full reign over customization, and you can secure your site to the hilt. Actually, you can host as many of your own sites as you desire on a dedicated server, if you have multiple sites. Once your website starts to receive a lot traffic, consider getting a dedicated server to your site with more security, stability, flexibility and dependability than a standard shared hosting service.

Colocated Hosting

Colocated hosting (sometimes written as "collocated") is where you purchase your own server, and have it hosted on a third party web host's data center. With colocated hosting, you are responsible for the actual server itself. An advantage of this type of hosting service is that you retain full control over everything. This is an extremely expensive option, reserved for those who are very sophisticated when it comes to server administration. The difference between colocated hosting and dedicated hosting is that with the former, you would have to purchase the server hardware, which can be costly.

The reason I'm telling you about colocated hosting, even though you're probably nowhere near choosing this as an option, is so that you can show off to your fellow online entrepreneurs that you know a few things about web hosting. When you can start dropping words like, "colocated hosting" at parties, people are impressed.

For now, I recommend you go with a shared hosting service. Just be sure it has the bandwidth and security levels that your website needs and your business deserves. Before choosing a web host, be sure to talk to someone in customer service who will answer all your questions, but don't rely on them to tell you how reliable their service is. Look out for red flags: If a web hosting company wants you to commit to a lengthy contract period (more than 6 months), proceed with caution. Money back guarantees are a good sign that the company takes your need for reliability seriously. Also, ask if you'll be charged more if your traffic increases beyond certain limits. Perhaps more importantly, ask around. Ask your fellow coaches if they are happy with their web hosting service.

Lastly, build a very simple website. Trust me, you're going to want to change it in six months anyway (if you're anything like I was when I first started out). You can have a website built for as little as $500 (what my developer charges for first-time websites), and it can look clean and simple and professional. And if money is a real concern, go to wordpress.org and learn how to do it yourself. Wordpress even has free themes available right out of the gate. Check out Youtube videos on how to build a website yourself using Wordpress.

ACTION STEPS:

1. Choose a website platform.

2. Choose a web host.

3. Pick a theme (keep it simple).

4. Build it (or have it built).

5. Launch that baby!

STEP 35: PREPARE YOUR WEBSITE'S LEGAL DOCS

There are 4 "foundational legal documents" (the bare-bones legal basics) that you need to have in place in order to cover your assets online once your website goes live.

1. Privacy Policy

The moment you start collecting emails on your website is the exact same moment you must post a privacy policy on said website.

It's the law.

You don't have to be selling anything. As soon as you ask someone for any type of personal information (name or email address, that's all it takes) you *must* tell them exactly what you will do with the information you're collecting, where you will keep that information, and how you will protect it.

Furthermore, your Privacy Policy must be prominently displayed on your website.

Why? Because it is there to protect the privacy of visitors to your website, and you must make it easy for visitors to know what they can expect from you when it comes to collecting sensitive information.

Don't make the mistake of simply cutting and pasting someone else's Privacy Policy onto your site. First of all, that's copyright infringement, with the lawyer that drafted the doc being the copyright owner. Importantly, you do need to make sure the document is tailored to your site and your business. I once reviewed someone else's Privacy Policy and it was loaded with mistakes, including specifying the wrong state in which the was registered to do business!

Remember, the FTC requires online entrepreneurs to post a Privacy Policy that adheres to their guidelines, including COPPA-the Children's Online Privacy Protection Act. Also, beware of CalOPPA—the California Online Privacy Protection Act. If any of your website visitors are from California, and they probably are or will be, you need to be aware of CalOPPA. If you are a California-based company, know that California has some of the strictest privacy protection requirements in the country—make sure you know them. As you can see, when it comes to a Privacy Policy, one size does not fit all.

2. Website Disclaimer

The main purpose of a website disclaimer is to limit a website owner's liability by letting people know that the information provided must not be improperly relied upon. You're telling visitors that you will not be held responsible for how they use or misuse the information on your site. Basically, it lets people know the nature of the content, its purpose, and what it is **and is not** intended for, which makes it a necessary foundational document on which to build your website.

A Website Disclaimer doesn't eliminate liability altogether, but it can go a long way towards minimizing your risk of exposure. Display your Website Disclaimer prominently in the footer of your site so that it shows up on every page.

The types of liability that website owners may have to contend with include negligence actions, libel/defamation allegations, copyright and trademark infringement, and breach of privacy. Most jurisdictions place limits on the effects of disclaimers and exclusions of liability. In other words, a Website Disclaimer won't protect you against all your mistakes, but it will go a long way toward protecting you from people who are trolling the web for targets, i.e., websites without these sort of protective policies in place.

3. Website Terms and Conditions Statement

Your website's Terms and Conditions Statement lets people know the rules they must follow if they want to use the content you provide on your site, as well as what they are not permitted to do (for example, copying and redistributing the content you provide). This is important, because it not only protects your intellectual property—your content— but your personal brand, and that's your biggest asset of all. This is your playground, your rules. Make sure you're very clear about what's allowed and what isn't, especially with regards to your copyrighted and trademarked material.

4. Products and Services Terms of Use

This document aims to limit your liability when it comes to your paid products and services. It warns against misuse of your products and services, and it also disclaims any liability that may arise out of such misuse. In other words, it helps you set out the rules and guidelines that your buyers must agree to in order to use your products and services. It puts the responsibility for success on the shoulders of the purchaser. It makes clear, for example, that your coaching products and services are not intended as a substitute for professional health care or to treat any mental illness or disease. It's best to have this documented included on your sales page as a link that is prominently displayed. You can also require that your buyers check a box confirming they've read this document *before* being allowed to purchase your products and services.

I don't want to scare you, really I don't. But as online entrepreneurs, we must take care of ourselves; we must protect our businesses (and our personal assets) ferociously. You don't want to put all that hard work into growing a successful online business and then have it all come crashing down because you didn't take the necessary steps to make sure your legal ducks and docs were all lined up in a nice little row.

I know. Some of this can be a royal pain in the "assets"... but your assets (everything you've created for your business) are worth it, right?

Of course!

This is not something to put off until you "get around to it." Because the last thing you *ever* want to hear is, *"You've been served."* You'll *never* have time for *that.*

ACTION STEPS:

1. Be wary of do-it-yourself products—hire a lawyer to help you with legal docs that are customized to your business.

2. Post these docs on your website, *stat!*

If you want help with preparing your website's legal docs, visit CoverYourAssetsOnline.com to review your options.

STEP 36: CREATE A MARKETING FUNNEL

Your marketing funnel is simply a progressive set of steps a prospective client will go through before they eventually become a buyer. The widest part of the funnel represents all the people who have taken you up on your free offer. As the funnel narrows, fewer people will be willing to move through to the next step (an introductory paid offer) and even fewer who will be willing to pay for your more expensive offers. As the funnel narrows, the more the "touch factor" increases, i.e., the closer your clients get to work with you, which coincides with a higher price point and higher expectations of your time. The clients making that investment will be your ideal clients, and it is for these people that you develop the funnel itself. Everything you offer is intended to attract your favorite clients.

Your website's Home Page represents the big, wide mouth of the funnel where your irresistible free opt-in awaits . Once your

LIN M. ELEOFF

funnel is set up, it's your job to keep sending as many new people as possible through the funnel.

A funnel can have many steps, but it will basically look like this:

Your Client's Journey With You

1. RECEIVE FREE OFFER + FOLLOW-UP CONTENT VIA EMAIL

2. SIGN UP FOR AMAZING INTRODUCTORY OFFER

3. WORK 1:1 WITH YOU

Funnel Step 1: Visitors to your website sign up for your amazing free content.

Funnel Step 2: You send follow up emails providing value and establishing a connection.

Funnel Step 3: Subscriber signs up for coaching session because they think you're awesome!

Of course, this is a very basic funnel. As your business grows, so will your funnel, with more steps representing the various

162

ways people can work with you, all while taking your customers on a valuable *experience* that builds and makes them want to keep investing in the relationship.

ACTION STEPS:

1. Take the time now to draw your marketing funnel so that you have a clear idea of the journey you want to take your visitors on when they go to your website.

2. Determine how many emails you will send and what they will contain.

3. Determine what you will offer for sale, and when, and what will be your high-touch offering, where you clients get to work closely with you.

STEP 37: WRITE YOUR WEBSITE'S MAIN PAGES

There are **five main pages** you must have on your website, and they should appear in the navigation bar of your site's header.

1. Home Page

2. About Page

3. Work With Me Page

4. Blog Directory Page

5. Contact Page

Home Page

In Step 20 I discussed the important elements of a Landing Page, and the same "rules" do apply, more or less, to your Home Page. However, the Home Page isn't as important as it once was. A lot of that has to do with a change in online search behavior. Often a new visitor will land on one of your website's pages through various links they find via search engines, social media, recommendations and endorsements, email and newsletters, and a host of other channels. If those deeper web pages are keeping visitors interested, it's likely they will eventually click on 'Home' in the nav bar and that's where you get to work some of your magic.

So while it may not always be the first stop for visitors to your site, it's still a valuable piece of real estate and one worth giving some extra attention to.

Gone are the days when a Home Page included *everything*—cluttered pages with multiple clickable options have become a turn-off for most people. Keep your Home Page simple, uncluttered, and to the point. This is your front door and an opportunity to introduce yourself in a way that will create a spark for your visitors—like when you meet someone for the first time at a party and you say to yourself, *I'd like to get to know her better.* While design is important (it is a reflection and an extension of your brand, after all), content is *more* important. The purpose of your Home Page is to convert visitors into leads, i.e., people who are willing to give you their email address in exchange for something you have that they want, so you want to make a good first impression, and you want to make it clear what you want your visitors to do: sign up for your free offer!

Here's are the main elements of a Home Page that converts:

- *Headline:* In as few words as possible, let people know what the website is about.

- *Sub-headline:* Let people know what problem you can solve for them.

- *Pro photo of you: no backyard shots please!*

LIN M. ELEOFF

- *Call to action promoting your free offer:* Make sure this appears above the fold and that it's a compelling offer directly related to your sub-headline.

- *Benefits of working with you (your promise):* Tell them how their lives will change if they hang out with you.

- *Testimonial(s):* If you have them, share at least one endorsement on your home page as social proof that you can be trusted to do what you say you can do.

One other option you have for your Home Page is to make it double as your Blog Directory Page. This is a good idea for some because it automatically updates the content on your Home Page on a regular basis. You can have it set up so that the latest post is featured in full and snippets of subsequent posts are highlighted with accompanying photos or graphic images. Just be sure it also includes the other main elements of the Home Page, as listed above, especially your free opt-in.

About Page

The About page is often the most read page on a website. I know that's where I tend to click whenever I find myself on someone else's site, especially if it's someone I don't know much about yet.

Your main goals here? 1) To make a statement and, 2) To make a connection. This is all about inviting your reader to connect with you by showing her what you both have in common.

Before you start writing your About Page, conjure up one person. It may be a previous client, or someone you'd love to work with. Keep them in mind as you write this page. This will help you remember that it's not about you, it's about the person who's going to be reading it. If you had ideas of cutting and pasting your CV here, that would be a big, giant no-no. No one will read it, and no one will see themselves in your story.

The first thing you want to convey is empathy. You want the reader to know you understand them because you've been exactly where they are, or you've helped people who have been where they are. This is often where the relationship with your reader begins and all they really care about is whether you have a solution to the problem they're struggling with. It's all about them at this point. Rather than giving information about you, you want to stir up *feelings* in them in order to make an emotional connection.

This is one place where you don't want to sit on the fence. Pick a side. Take a stand. Make a statement that demands attention. The people who are on your side will stick with you. The others will leave. You want that.

Show your personality. Use your charm. Brag a little, if that's your style. *Show* who you are in the way you talk to your reader, not by *telling* them who you are.

There's an art to writing an About Page, so be patient. Write it yourself and if necessary, get some help from a copywriter. This page is important and you want to be sure to get it right. Show it to trusted friends who won't be afraid to give you honest feedback.

Include another picture of yourself on this page, one that conveys the words you've written, all in a single image.

Work With Me Page

This page is where you invite people to take *the next step* in your marketing funnel. Hopefully they've already signed up for your free offer. If that offer is a simple download, you might consider offering a free mini-session right here on your Work With Me Page. It really does depend on where you are as far as list-building goes. If you're just starting out, those free mini-sessions can work wonders if done properly.

Like the other pages on your website, you want to keep this one simple.

Focus.

What is it you want people to do here? If helpful, apply the principles outlined in Step 40, how to write a killer sales page.

And, remember the person you conjured up when you were writing your About Page? Keep her in mind as you write your WWM Page. Tell her what the next step is. If your main goal is to get her to sign up for a free session, then focus on how she'll benefit from that. If it's to get her to sign up for your introductory program, then focus on that.

Whatever you do on this page, sell one thing, and make sure it's not your *one big thing.* That's reserved for people who already know how amazing you are as a coach because they've worked with you. Those who are just learning about you don't want to risk spending a lot of money on someone they don't know yet.

If you're just starting out and building a list from scratch, your main focus is not so much on sales but in building that list of your faithful followers; people you'd love to work with, people who might also know others who would love to test-drive one of your mini sessions. On the other hand, if you've been at this for a while, and you've expanded your marketing funnel, you may choose to present visitors with three or four options for how they can work with you, depending on how well they already know you. You might offer a $97 product, a $297 product, a $497 group program, and a higher-ticket one-on-one package for $997. When you do this, you're also creating what's called an "anchoring effect," which makes people more readily buy the lower priced products, because they're perceived as a good value as compared to the higher priced ones.

Blog Directory Page

This page is pretty straight forward. When you click on "blog" in the navigation bar, it takes you to a page that lists all your blog posts, with the most current being at the top. You get to decide how much of a "snippet" you show of each post. It can be a few lines or several paragraphs. The reader then clicks on "read more" to continue to the full post. It's common to include images on this page as well. Depending on the layout of your website, it's a good idea to include your free opt-in here or at the bottom of each blog post.

Contact Page

Your readers may have questions, so you want to make it easy for them to contact you. Let them know you welcome their questions, comments, and concerns—and give them an easy way to contact you, preferably with a built-in contact form that your web designer can install for you, although many themes include this feature already.

Have the form go to a specified email address that you're sure not to miss. The last thing you want is to have someone reach out to you and you miss that email entirely.

ACTION STEPS:

Using the above guidelines, write each of the following:

1. Your Home Page copy

2. Your About Page copy

3. Your Work With Me Page copy

4. Your Contact Page

5. Upload all of the above to your website

6. Add photos of you!

LIN M. ELEOFF

STEP 38: BE (EXTRA) CAREFUL WITH IMAGES

Royalty free. Public domain. Fair use.

These terms are often mistaken by coaches wanting to use images on their websites and throughout their products and services. And that's a mistake that can cost you BIG!

"Royalty free" does NOT mean the images are altogether "free" to use.

Just because it's on the Internet or on Google doesn't mean in it's in the "public domain."

And "fair use" doesn't mean what YOU think is fair.

ROYALTY FREE images are those for which you have purchased a license granting you certain rights; the cost of the license will depend on the scope of the rights you purchase. "Royalty free" simply means you don't have to pay every time you use the photo; you have unlimited use for a specified period of time.

PUBLIC DOMAIN images are non-copyrighted and can be copied and freely used *but not sold.* No permission or payment is required. All copyrighted work eventually enters

172

the public domain. Anything published before 1923 is part of the public domain. After that, things get complicated because the law has changed several times.

Just be extremely careful, read the fine print, and assume nothing. Infringing on someone else's copyright is costing online entrepreneurs thousands of dollars every day. Stock image companies are watching and they are sending out demand letters to anyone who uses their images without paying for that use. And they have every right to collect from you.

Oh, and simply giving attribution doesn't count, no matter how fair you think that may be.

The best assumption you can ever make is that if it's not yours— if you didn't create it— or you didn't purchase the rights to use it, then you likely have *no legal right* to post it on your website or anywhere else unless it truly is in the public domain.

Same goes for images that appear on Pinterest and Instagram— they are not presumptively part of the public domain. You can't get around it by giving credit or attribution to the photographer or graphic artist. It's still copyright infringement. That's because it's not up to you to decide whether the image can be used, it's up to the artist. And don't assume you're doing them a favor by giving them "exposure." Get written permission, and/or negotiate a payment. The last thing you want is to be facing a lawsuit. Those stock image companies are ruthless. Do not mess with them.

ACTION STEPS:

1. Find a source for free public domain images online (ex. Unsplash) but pay very close attention to the rights and whether it's a "zero commons" license (allowing you full rights).

2. Find a royalty free (paid) source for images (always read the license's fine print!).

3. Create your own graphics using Canva or PicMonkey or Photoshop.

STEP 39: CREATE YOUR FIRST PROGRAM OR PRODUCT

This doesn't have to be elaborate when you're first starting out. In fact, the simpler the better, because as you and your business grow, your products will undergo several iterations.

Here is the quickest way to create a coaching program, whether it's for one-on-one coaching or for a group (you can keep the price lower if you can get a group together).

ACTION STEPS:

1. Assuming you've got a clearly defined niche (if not, go back to Step 4), identify six topics that your clients typically struggle with and the corresponding solutions/tools you have created (or are about to create) to help them solve their problem. If this is difficult, speak to your clients... or conduct a survey. The more you know and understand your clients, the easier this will be. If you're struggling with this first step, you may need more clarity regarding your niche.

2. Next, arrange the topics in a way that shows progression over a six-week period.

3. Create an outline for how you would teach/coach your clients on each topic and give each topic a creative name.

4. Create 2-3 specific exercises for each topic and turn them into worksheets.

5. Come up with a creative name for your six-week program.

6. Put a price on it—one that's irresistible.

7. Consider offering the program for free or for a very reduced price in order to fill seats. Trust me it will be worth it—you're going to learn so much from this process and you'll likely be able to collect several testimonials to help you sell the program next time around.

8. When you run the program, record it. Make sure you have signed permission from those who are on the call, and let them know you may be re-using the material for future programs. Use the recordings and worksheets to create a stand-alone "evergreen" product. Consider pricing it somewhere between $47 to $97 or whatever feels "right" to you (see following steps). You can then add this to your product suite.

STEP 40: DESIGN A KILLER SALES PAGE

I cannot stress this enough... the more you know your target market and your ideal client, the easier it will be to write your website copy, blog posts, create products, and write a sales page that will attract paying clients. You should know your potential clients so well that they will truly think you're able to read their minds.

For example, your ideal client may think she has a problem losing weight. As a coach, you know that there's a lot more going on than being able to lose weight. But if you try to sell someone on changing their thoughts or getting in touch with their emotions, you may lose her. That's *your* language, not hers. How often do you hear someone say, *"I really need to change the way I think about losing weight"?*

Instead, they're saying other things, depending on how old they are, how much they have to lose, whether they've always been overweight, or if it's something that happened after an event like having a baby. If you're not intimately tuned in to what they're thinking and worrying about, they'll pass you by.

Your sales page needs to convey that you understand how much this means to your visitors and that you have answers they haven't heard before.

You also have to know the personality of your prospective clients; are they fun-loving or very serious? This will certainly affect how you write your copy. Consider, too, if they like to work one-on-one or in a group.

ACTION STEPS:

Make sure to include these key components of an effective sales page:

1. **Write An Eye-Catching Headline:** This needs to pre-qualify the reader of your sales page. If your product is geared to women over 40, make that clear right off the top. If you dilute it, no one will pay attention. The headline must make a promise that is both attention grabbing and *believable*. For example: *"Ready to lose the baby weight?"* is obviously geared to women who've just had children, rather than, *"Ready to lose weight?"* which speaks to everyone... and no one.

2. **Tease Them With Your Offer:** In the first paragraph under the headline you want to draw the reader in, letting them know you know exactly what it's like to be in their shoes. You want to establish a connection so that they'll want to keep reading. *"I know the feeling. After I had my second baby I couldn't seem to lose the weight no matter what I tried. I did this, I did that, to no avail..."* You're not talking about your own product, you're talking about them, even when you're talking about you.

3. **Focus On The Benefits:** Put yourself in the reader's shoes. Weave your story into the copy so that it's almost hard to tell whether you're talking about you or you're talking about the reader. Talk about your product but focus on *benefits*, not

features. People pay for benefits, meaning, the transformation that you're promising. While the features are important, don't make them the focus of your pitch. Of course, people will want to know all about the features, i.e., the number of modules, phone calls, worksheets, etc., but this isn't what they're *buying.* They're buying the promise you're making. They're buying their future transformation. Sell them that in a way that is authentic and from your heart and people will buy your programs, products, and services.

4. **Establish Authority and Credibility:** You want to tell the reader what qualifies you to offer this course but you don't want it to sound like a resume. Instead of, "I am a master certified life coach," you'll want to say, "When I became a life coach..." or "Life coaching has taught me..." or even, "My unique set of life coaching tools has helped my clients achieve..." You want to pique the reader's interest, while also letting them know you know *what* the "real" problem is, not *how* to solve it—that's what they get when they sign up to work with you. Establish yourself as an authoritative source of information and a coach who gets results.

5. **Use Testimonials:** If used the right way, testimonials can sell your product for you. They're the "proof" that it actually works. Make sure to clearly identify the person who is endorsing you, using a first and last name and a photo if at all

possible. The testimonial should explain how the person was changed after having gone through your program. This can really help to establish your authority and credibility.

Use testimonials to answer objections that the reader is likely raising in her mind, such as, *"How do I know this will work for me since nothing else has?"* The purpose of a testimonial is twofold: First, it lets the reader know that people have succeeded by using your program; secondly, but most importantly, it immediately reduces the reader's ongoing sense of angst over their problem. It gives them hope that maybe, just maybe, this will work.

6. Design Your Page Using White Space, Headings and Images: Your sales page must be visually appealing and easy on the eyes. There's nothing worse than having to read endless paragraphs of copy. In fact, chances are, no one will bother. Make sure to break up the text with catchy headings that allow the reader to skim, yet still understand the story in just a few minutes. Leave lots of white space. Consider using relevant images and graphics that break up the text and add visual context and design.

7. Put A Price Tag On It: First of all, stop cringing! Pricing your product need not make you squirm. By now, if you're not convinced your product is full of value and worth paying for, no one else will, that's certain. I want you to be excited about your product—that's the energy your prospects are going to pick up on and make them want to buy in. Put a price on it that's enticing, yet doesn't diminish how you feel about you. (Step 41 goes into pricing further.) Reiterate how your program is different from others they may have seen or tried, and how much they will benefit from yours. Explain how this investment in themselves will reap rewards that will last a lifetime. Invite them on an adventure like nothing they've ever experienced before.

8. **Close The Sale:** You never have to use the word "buy" if you don't want to. There are so many courses out there about how to sell without sounding "sales-y" but the truth is this: You *are* selling something. You also want people to buy what you're selling, and that's only a bad thing if your mind keeps telling you it is. Sometimes I think closing the sale requires convincing the seller (you) first... because the buyer can only be ready when you are.

9. **End With A Strong Call To Action:** Make it obvious what needs to happen next. They need to click a "buy" button. This is the exclamation point of your sales page. Make it easy for them to find because, if you've done everything else right, they'll be looking for it.

STEP 41: PRICE YOUR PRODUCTS, PROGRAMS AND SERVICES FEARLESSLY!

Pricing your products may put you back into The Land of WTF more times than you'd like to admit. It's quite possibly The One Big Thing that trips us up when we offer our products, programs, and services, especially when we're first starting out. Trust me, you can do this by following this simple formula to get started:

1. Determine your hourly rate, let's say for simplicity's sake it's $100.

2. How many hours will you be teaching and coaching live on a call? Let's say it's once a week for 6 weeks. 6 hours x $100 = $600.

3. If you bust your butt and get 6 people to sign up for your class you could charge $97 and get paid, at least, for the time you spend on the coaching calls.

A price point like $97 for a group program being offered for the first time is not unreasonable, and I wouldn't suggest going any lower. At least that will pay for your live coaching calls with the group. Chalk up the rest of the time you spent working on the program as time invested in growing your business. You'll learn so much from the entire experience of offering your first program.

I want you to be excited about selling your products and services. For example, when I created my DIY Legal Toolkit, (DIYLegalTookkit.com), I was absolutely *convinced beyond measure* that it was going to help online business owners more than they could ever realize. I know in my heart that it is full of value because I put my *heart and soul* into that product. I really did. I loved creating it, even the design. I imagined how much my clients were going to breathe such a sigh of relief when they opened it up and saw that it answered so many questions. I also knew it would provide answers to important questions they didn't even know to ask. And they would be impressed beyond their expectations and know they got a lot of value from it.

I was aware of a problem coaches were having: how to build an online business, step-by-step, and protect it, legally. I knew that online business owners wanted to feel a sense of security regarding their personal assets, but they didn't want to spend a ton of money on legal fees, at least not in the early stages of their businesses. I wanted to create a product that would help them solve their "problem" without having to hire a lawyer.

Ultimately, what I'm selling with the DIY Legal Toolkit is that feeling of *ahhhhhhhhhhh*—the relief we feel when we've found something that is truly going to help us. And the toolkit absolutely helps coaches and other online entrepreneurs finally do something that will make them feel more in control of their businesses and their personal assets. I'm selling security and, as much as I hate to use this word too often, *empowerment.* I knew the risks involved in not taking action when it comes to the "legal stuff." I also knew there was resistance to paying for the legal stuff. So I created a product that solved the problem. Voila, the DIY Legal Toolkit was born, and I'm not afraid to charge for it because I know its real value is immeasurable. Not only does it save people thousands of dollars in legal fees, it could save them from being on the receiving end of a lawsuit, or from having their content stolen.

Oh no. I'm not afraid to put a price tag on that baby.

That's how I want you to feel about your products and services.

Keep in mind that the more people you have on your list, the higher you can price your products and services, *but only if it feels good to do so.* I've heard some "experts" tell people to raise their prices higher and higher "just because." I disagree. And, as a coach, I'm sure you're going to want to price your products in a way that feels right. Whatever you decide, do it fearlessly.

ACTION STEPS:

1. Determine your hourly rate.

2. Determine how many hours you want to work each day/week.

3. Do the math to determine what you need to charge for your products and services so that you recoup your hourly rate, at least for the time spent actually coaching.

STEP 42: GET A SIGNED CLIENT SERVICES AGREEMENT

There's one big reason why you need to get a signed agreement from each of your clients:

You are worth it. And so is your business.

Think of your Client Services Agreement (CSA) as a virtual boundary that protects you *and your client* from the unknown. The agreement identifies what the coach will—and will not—do for the client. I can almost see some of you squirming at the thought of having to give this to your clients.

But, is it really that necessary? (Yes.)

It feels so... legal. (And that's bad because...?)

What if they get mad at me and cancel?" (Coach thyself in the *extreme*, please.)

Isn't it overkill? (No. No. No. No. No. No. No. No. No. Although saying 'no' that many times might be considered overkill.)

And, by the way, saying, *"It'll never happen to me"* is tantamount to putting your head in the sand and pretending it's not your head.

Remember, it's all about how you choose to think about this or any other piece of your business. And think about this: without a CSA, what will you do when your client cancels an hour, or even 5 minutes before a session—or worse, doesn't show up for the call at all? Or if she insists you agreed to provide email coaching on a daily basis, including weekends?

A Client Services Agreement defines the terms of the coaching relationship, thereby preventing misunderstandings between coach and client. It also provides possible remedies should you discover, after the relationship starts, that this isn't such a great fit after all.

Your agreement should be tailored to your business and the program you're offering. Still, there are some important terms that should be included:

1. A clear description of the services provided by the coach;

2. Fees and payment terms;

3. An explanation of the coach-client relationship;

4. Cancellation, refund, and termination policies;

5. Confidentiality expectations;

6. How disputes between the parties will be mediated;

7. Limitations on the coach's liability;

8. Other standard boilerplate language.

Fortunately you can your client sign the agreement electronically. Digital signatures are legally binding. Electronic signature companies make it easy for you to send contracts. Google "electronic signatures" and choose from a host of services, some of them free. Have your client sign the doc first, and then you sign and send a copy. And, if it helps, you can send the CSA to your client with the attached note:

Dear Client,

I am including a link to my Client Services Agreement for you to sign electronically. How cool is it that we don't have to do this by snail mail!? It's a document that spells out in detail the coaching program you signed up for and how we'll work together over the next _____ weeks/months. It also assures you of the confidentiality of our relationship, and provides terms that help both of us, such as what to do if either of us needs to cancel. Please read it over and let me know if you have any questions. Once it's signed we are off to the races! I'm so excited to be working with you.

Sincerely,

[Your name]

The Best Coach, EVER!

ACTION STEPS:

You can have a lawyer draft a CSA for you or you can do it yourself following the detailed instructions and template I include in my **DIY Legal Toolkit** (<u>DIYLegalToolkit.com</u>). Once you have your agreement written, you can take it to a lawyer in your state and have her review it for a fraction of what it would cost you to have it done for you from scratch.

STEP 43: OFFER FREE MINI SESSIONS TO ATTRACT 1:1 CLIENTS

If your free offer isn't converting your website visitors into leads, you might consider offering free one-on-one mini coaching sessions. Notice I said "*coaching* sessions." This is not supposed to be a pitch fest where you talk about your products and services. In fact, you shouldn't mention anything about working with you on a deeper level or your offerings or any other aspect of your business. This is all about your client and how you can help her in just 15 minutes.

A mini-session is intended to show your clients how one particular thought or belief is causing so much of their pain.

The trick is to be able to find that painful thought or belief in the first 5 minutes (you can send pre-work to help start things off), show them how it's creating unnecessary suffering in the next 6 or 7 minutes, and in the final few minutes, give them an easy tool to try out as "homework." This gives you an opportunity to follow up with them via email to see how they're doing and to keep the conversation going.

You want to create a new relationship with this person. When you build *relationships* in business it never feels like "work." So make sure you ditch the pitch whenever you're doing a mini-session and make it clear that you won't be selling them anything on the call. They'll be quite surprised when you keep your word.

After you follow up on their homework and answer any questions they may have, invite them back on the phone to talk about how much more you can help them. If they agree to another call, use the time to explain to them how the coaching process works and how you believe your program can help them. This is not a time to give them more (free) coaching. This is a time to connect **connect** *connect* with them. When you do this right, you never have to *sell anything.*

I practice this a lot with my coach clients until they can do it in15-20 minutes. The key is to identify and then focus on one small and very particular thought pattern and show your prospective client how it's affecting the way they feel on a day to day basis.

The better you get at this, the more success you'll have at getting people to sign up to work with you.

ACTION STEPS:

1.   Offer a free mini-coaching session to at least <u>ten</u> people.

2.   Repeat step 1 until you have booked all your available time slots for the next four weeks.

3.   Repeat step 2. (This works!)

STEP 44: GET TESTIMONIALS

We all know how powerful a testimonial can be. It can make people want to instantly sign up for your products and services.

There's nothing like "social proof" to improve your "Know-Like-Trust" factor. The higher your KLT, the more people will be eager to work with you.

So... what makes a testimonial powerful? That's easy.

The Truth. That's it.

If it's truth-*full* then it will naturally be a powerful testament to what you can do for your clients and customers. Besides, when you don't stick to the truth you may raise the ire of the FTC, the government body charged with protecting consumers. "Unfair and deceptive practices" are not allowed and the FTC has beefed up its laws requiring truth in advertising, and testimonials fall under the category of advertising.

Here are the elements of a powerful, effective testimonial:

- It's not flowery or gushy, a.k.a. fake;

- It's written the way people talk;

- It provides answers to the objections people are quietly thinking to themselves, *"What makes her different from any other lawyer out there?" "Why should I pay that much for something like this?" "What if it doesn't work?"* If that's what people are already thinking, your copy must address their concerns, and doing so via a testimonial is more effective than doing it yourself.

- It paints a clear "before and after" picture of how your clients have been transformed by using your product or service;

- It's a *real person* with a first AND last name, a photo, and maybe a website URL.

Testimonials don't have to necessarily be written word. They can be also be videotaped or voice recorded.

Finally, be absolutely certain you have permission to use the testimonial as well as the person's personally identifiable information, including (especially) their photo. Don't open yourself up to a lawsuit for a breach of their right to privacy. It can be as simple as keeping the email in which they consented as proof.

If someone says "no" to allowing their name to be published, find someone else. First-name only, or initials-only, or otherwise anonymized testimonials always look suspect, even if they're real.

ACTION STEPS:

1. Create a process for collecting testimonials after you work with a client or a group.

2. Write out a series of questions such that the answers will provide a clear picture of the transformation they experienced after working with you.

3. Use first and last names (with permission) and a photo if possible.

4. Make sure you get it in writing that they agree to your using the testimonial on your website and in other promotion material.

STEP 45: TAKE CYBER SECURITY MEASURES

The Internet has allowed businesses of all sizes from around the world to reach new and expanded markets. Small businesses, like the one you're building, are able to serve clients from across the country and often in other parts of the world. Cyber security is about protecting businesses and their computers, computer networks, computer programs, and computer data from all sorts of bad things that can happen on the Internet, including unauthorized access to protected information, as well as the disclosure or the destruction of that information.

Whether you use cloud computing, or are just using email and maintaining a website, cyber security should be of great concern because theft of digital information has now surpassed physical theft as the most commonly reported fraud.

Besides, you are responsible for creating a culture of security in your business that will make visitors to your website feel safe and confident that you are able to keep cyberspace hooligans and scallawags at bay.

ACTION STEPS:

1. Take stock of your assets and who has access to them, especially when it comes to your website. Talk to your web host about security measures they have in place to prevent attacks from hackers and malicious codes.

2. Keep track of the kind of data you collect from clients and visitors to your site. Make sure you have a Privacy Policy posted on your website.

3. Provide extra layers of security, including passwords and encryption codes to protect sensitive data.

4. Plan for the unexpected. Back up your data! Should your information ever be hijacked by hackers, or even accidentally erased, you must have a backup copy!

5. Beware of "phishing." Phishing is a scam used by online criminals to trick people into thinking they are dealing with a trusted website or company. Phishing can come at you from two directions: Phishers may impersonate you in order to take advantage of your unsuspecting customers. They may also steal the online credentials of people who work for you in an effort to pry sensitive information from you that you would not normally share.

6. Don't fall for anti-virus scams. Fake antivirus "scareware" and other online security scams have been behind some of the most successful online frauds in recent history. Do not respond to dire warnings that your computer has been compromised and is about to blow up.

7. Beware of spyware and adware. When installed on your computer (without your even being aware of it) spyware and adware will cause pop-up ads to appear on your screen, redirect you to websites other than what you typed in your browser, and will keep track of websites you visit and can leave you vulnerable to privacy theft.

STEP 46: JOIN A MASTERMIND

If you want to grow your business, you simply must be a in a mastermind group, even if it's made up of only two people (3 to 5 is ideal). You need others to bounce your ideas off of and to exchange the latest programs and tools that will help you run your business more effectively. It's also helpful for when you have a sticky situation with a client or a coaching issue you need guidance with. This is your sounding board, not your water cooler.

Every successful online business owner I know readily admits that they owe much of their success to masterminding.

My first mastermind was made up of three coaches with whom I went through coach training. It was very supportive and helped me immensely when I first started my business. I eventually joined a high-level mastermind group and am now in my third year. Sometimes it feels like I'm swimming with sharks. And let me tell you, there are quite a few Great Whites in this sea of high achievers. That's the best part; there's so much to learn from people who have achieved success and are willing to share it with you. At the same time, be sure to contribute to the group and offer value in your own areas of expertise.

LIN M. ELEOFF

Not sure how to find a mastermind group? Ask around. I have a private (free) mastermind group just for coaches on Facebook. You can find it by going to GutsyGlorious.com—it'll take you straight to FB. You can also form your own mastermind by rounding up your fellow coaches, and be sure to mix it up—invite people with different backgrounds and levels of expertise; that way you'll have a lot to learn from each other.

ACTION STEPS:

1. Choose 3-5 people for the group—they don't all have to be a coaches.

2. Decide the format of the calls (ex.,10 minutes each followed by general discussion of a hot topic).

3. Have weekly or bi-weekly meetings—this helps with accountability and momentum.

4. Make sure everyone is committed to showing up on schedule and on time because the group is counting on each other for support.

ON BEING A GOOD BOSS

Repeat after me: *"I will be a good boss and treat my favorite employee (me!) with utmost love and respect and gratitude for the hard work she does every day."*

Let's face it: going into business can be both exhilarating and terrifying. On the one hand, you're in charge of creating and fulfilling the vision; on the other hand, it's a lot of hard work and there are no guarantees of how it will turn out.

The tricky part is to not become a lousy boss to yourself: the kind that over-works you, mistreats you, makes you start early in the morning and work late into the night; the kind of boss that insists family—and fun—will just have to wait. The kind that thinks you have to do everything on your own, because no one else can do it like you.

So stop right now and think about the kind of boss you want to have bossing you around.

Here are some of the tell-tale signs that you may have to have a meeting with your boss:

- You have no work schedule: Your family starts accusing you of being on the computer "all day long," even on the weekends.

- You start neglecting your health—your meals come in foil bags and are a bright orange color. (Doritos anyone?)

- You don't have repeatable systems and workflows. You scramble from project to project, and from task to task.

- You're easily distracted by your favorite social media platforms, which merely adds to the overwhelm you feel almost daily.

Consider this, from Michael Gerber, author of *The E-Myth Revisited*:

> *"With no clear picture of how you wish your life to be, how on Earth are you going to live it? What is your Primary Aim? Where is the script to make your dreams come true? What is the first step to take and how do you measure your progress? How far have you gone and how close are you to getting to your goals?"*

You see, Coach, there's no getting around it; a meaningful business, and for that matter, a meaningful life, always comes back to how well you understand *your Self*—showing up as *your Self,* honoring *your Self,* standing up for *your Self,* and, above all, being kind and compassionate towards *your Self.*

The moment you decided that you wanted to be your own boss, you unknowingly opened a door to the possibility of becoming the gutsiest, most glorious version of your Self.

'Cause you've got some serious guts, right Coach?

And you can already sense that your glory awaits.

Here's to doing *business at the speed of badass.*

I cannot wait to hear about your future successes.

OPTIONAL STEPS

If you get a thrill out of checking things off a list, make sure you get my free step-by-step checklist (with all 46 steps listed in this book) to help you stay on task. You can download it at GutsyGloriousLifeCoach.com. Also, be sure to check out my podcast, *"The Business of Being a Life Coach"* at GutsyGloriousRadio.com.

I realize that there's a lot of work ahead, especially if you're just getting started, but that's the reality of starting your own business and anyone who tells you otherwise is not being honest. The truth is, most people who read a how-to book don't ever really intend to take action; but you're not like "most people," right Coach?

If you'd like some support in implementing the 46 steps in this book, I'm ready for you. If it's coaching you want, go to LinEleoff.com. And if you're looking for help with the legal aspects of your business, visit me at CoverYourAssetsOnline.com.

Here's to your guts and the inevitable glory that is about to ensue,

Lin E.

ABOUT THE AUTHOR

What happens when a lawyer, a life coach, and an online business owner walk into a room?

Lin Eleoff is a lawyer who happens to be a life coach who also happens to be an online business woman. She's also an award-winning (former) television news reporter and anchor.

Combining all of the above has made Lin a go-to source for gutsy glorious women who want to turn it up a notch in all aspects of their lives: business, relationships, money, and, of course, weight and health, which she wrote about in her book, The Dignity Diet: How to End the Cycle of Cry-Eat-Repeat.

Lin lives in New England with her husband, whom she lovingly calls Thurston Howell the Fourth, and their four children.

Websites: LinEleoff.com
           GutsyGloriousLifeCoach.com
           CoverYourAssetsOnline.com

Podcast: GutsyGloriousRadio.com